Douglas M. Thornton

Trust
Or
Bust

How to Win by Building Trust in the Workplace

Douglas M. Thornton

Trust or Bust

Order this book online at www.trafford.com/08-0022
or email orders@trafford.com

Most Trafford titles are also available at major online book retailers.

© Copyright 2008 Douglas M. Thornton.

All rights reserved. No part of this publication may be reproduced, stored in a retrieval system, or transmitted, in any form or by any means, electronic, mechanical, photocopying, recording, or otherwise, without the written prior permission of the author.

Note for Librarians: A cataloguing record for this book is available from Library and Archives Canada at www.collectionscanada.ca/amicus/index-e.html

Printed in Victoria, BC, Canada.

ISBN: 978-1-4251-6819-3

We at Trafford believe that it is the responsibility of us all, as both individuals and corporations, to make choices that are environmentally and socially sound. You, in turn, are supporting this responsible conduct each time you purchase a Trafford book, or make use of our publishing services. To find out how you are helping, please visit www.trafford.com/responsiblepublishing.html

Our mission is to efficiently provide the world's finest, most comprehensive book publishing service, enabling every author to experience success. To find out how to publish your book, your way, and have it available worldwide, visit us online at www.trafford.com/10510

www.trafford.com

North America & international
toll-free: 1 888 232 4444 (USA & Canada)
phone: 250 383 6864 ♦ fax: 250 383 6804
email: info@trafford.com

The United Kingdom & Europe
phone: +44 (0)1865 722 113 ♦ local rate: 0845 230 9601
facsimile: +44 (0)1865 722 868 ♦ email: info.uk@trafford.com

10 9 8 7 6 5 4 3 2

For Anne Marie

Table of Contents

Preface _____ v

Chapter 1-- The Trust Principles _____ 1

Chapter 2-- Changing Organizational Culture 15

Chapter 3-- Problems in the Workplace _____ 18

Chapter 4-- The Trust Organization _____ 24

Chapter 5-- Trust Organization vs. An Average Organization _____ 27

Chapter 6-- The "Feel" of Trust _____ 345

Chapter 7-- The Good News: Workplace Trust Already Exists_____ 45

Chapter 8-- The Bad News: Barriers to Trust Exist_____ 58

Chapter 9-- Overcoming Communication Barriers_____ 73

Chapter 10-- Managing People _____ 102

Chapter 11-- Barriers to Trust: Lack of Personal Accountability _____ 126

Chapter 12-- Getting Started _____ 146

References _____ 161

Preface

> *"I came to see, in my time at IBM, that culture isn't just one aspect of the game – it is the game."*
>
> – Former IBM CEO Lou Gerstner

This book is aimed at helping you build trust within your organization.

Trustful, motivated staff will transform your organization into a positive, productive culture yielding industry-leading products and services.

Without trust, however, your organization will remain an average workplace with unengaged employees producing average results. You might survive for the next few years, but your organization is headed for disaster.

Where would you rather work?

Whether you are a leader, manager, supervisor or employee, know that each person plays an important role in creating an organizational culture where all can contribute, progress and enjoy success.

It doesn't matter what type of workplace it is; the principles discussed in this book apply equally to retail operations, family-owned businesses, medium-sized companies, NGOs, multinational corporations and government organizations.

Before I reveal these trust principles, however, take a moment to reflect on your organization's culture.

Are your co-workers always trustworthy, cooperative and striving toward the same goal? Do employees believe in the organization's leaders? If you work hard and add value to your organization, are you certain that your loyalty and contribution will be rewarded adequately?[1]

If you answered "yes" to these questions and the descriptions accurately reflect your workplace, congratulations – you need not read any further.

If, however, you are uncertain or you are thinking, "I wish our organization was like that," then you have found the right book. What is lacking – and what your organization desperately needs – is a workplace culture based on trust.

Searching for Trust

Most of us search for organizational trust all our professional lives. We cherish opportunities to work with people who are honest, trustworthy and equally committed to achieving quality outcomes. We seek out leaders who enable us to use our own judgment and allow us to do our job, our way. We happily give extraordinary efforts for bosses who create opportunities for us to earn trust and who acknowledge our hard work and dedication.

How often, however, do we find ourselves in these win-win situations? How many teams have you been on during your career that achieved outstanding results? How many bosses have you had that encouraged your talents, nurtured your skills and insisted you take credit for every success?

Hopefully, you have been on many productive teams and have had several great mentors. However, more likely you've answered "not often," "very few" or "never." You've likely experienced a few successes, a few disappointments and a whole lot of average.

You may not even be aware of what was missing from your organization's culture; your instincts told you when a workplace felt "right" or not. Whether you could identify it or not, it is the presence of trust – its principles and practices – that drive individuals and organizations to achieve outstanding results.[2] And it is the absence of trust that creates average organizations with average performance and an abundance of unengaged employees. In this era of global competition, constant innovation and labour shortages, "average" means "unable to compete."

Who Should Read This Book?

This book is for executives who want to build trust organizations, hone their leadership skills and achieve outstanding results. It is for managers desiring to improve communication skills, motivate employees and reduce workplace stress. This book is for employees seeking trustful work environments where they will flourish and fulfill their potential.

The Time for Change is NOW

It is the perfect time to change your organization's culture and create a healthier environment. Large numbers of Baby Boomers are retiring and with them, the old-style "command and control" management practices featuring rigid hierarchies and stifling bureaucracies. New technologies, an emphasis on learning environments and greater employee empowerment have allowed millions of young employees flooding into the workforce to make a fresh start.

This new generation of technologically advanced workers is looking for organizations that reward talent and offer a less stressful environment. With more job opportunities and career choices available than "Baby Boom echo" workers to fill them, it is truly a job seeker's market. Will these prospective employees choose to work in organizations that tolerate or reward toxic behaviours? Or will they seek out organizations encouraging trust, teamwork, cooperation and knowledge-sharing? Which would you choose?

Given the looming shortage of qualified workers, your organization must take the opportunity to improve its culture now. Why continue the status quo and reward practices that stress your workforce and fail to engage employees? Why pour time and money into another "employee renewal" campaign only to find that most staff view it cynically and regard it as condescending? Why spend millions of dollars on a management fad that will likely produce nothing of significance? Why hire people for their talent, then under-utilize that talent? Why spend good money trying to convince candidates that your organization is an "employer of choice" when it really isn't?

In an intensely competitive global marketplace, only organizations able to transform themselves into trust-based cultures will succeed in the next few decades. They will be more profitable, attract and retain the best staff and enjoy a positive workplace culture that sustains growth. All this is quite possible for your organization as soon as it begins to positively impact employee behaviour.

This book seeks to help you bring positive changes to your organization's culture. It's about building the kind of workplace trust where leaders communicate effectively, managers empower teams and employees bring 100 percent of themselves to work every day. It's about feeling positive about what you and your organization achieve. Most of all, it's about giving everyone in your organization opportunities that lead to progress, innovation and fulfillment.

> *"We are not interested in having miserable people work for us."*
>
> *- WestJet CEO Clive Beddoes*

A cautionary note: Organizational culture does not change overnight. Some bad habits take decades to eliminate.[3] Although it *is* possible to change bad habits the process must be organic, inclusive, modeled by leaders, rewarded by managers and rigidly followed by all employees. People not committed to positive changes in the organization need to be persuaded to alter their behaviours, or be encouraged to move on.

Having an organizational culture based on trust is indeed "the game" – and the difference between sustained success and inevitable failure.[4] It's trust or bust.

Chapter 1
The Trust Principles

Recently, a woman named Elaine attended one of our Building Workplace Trust© team building sessions. During a break, she called me over and asked if I knew the etymology of the word "trust." I had to admit that I did not.

"The Latin word for trust is *fides*, so that wasn't very helpful, and the Romance languages don't show a common root," she explained. "So I did some research and found that the word 'trust' is actually an Old or Middle English word meaning 'trussed'. When a bridge was built, trusses were used to support it. When someone successfully crossed the bridge several times, it was said to be a well 'trussed' bridge. In other words, it was something you could rely on. You'll notice that the word is also in the past tense, so it is based on something that you've experienced."

I thanked Elaine for her research and enlightening explanation.

The "Trust" Bridge

The more I thought about this, the more it struck me that the idea of building a well-"trussed" bridge was a fitting metaphor for building trust in the workplace. People arrive at work wanting to contribute. To move forward, employees need help overcoming a number of perceived barriers – a fear-based environment, a lack of information, conflicting priorities, etc. Effective organizations build "bridges" that enable employees to overcome these obstacles and make progress.

The seven principles contained in this book are designed to accomplish exactly that: build a bridge that helps employees overcome barriers and become more productive, happier and more engaged.

If an organization's culture is characterized by trust, employees bring all their ideas, enthusiasm and skills to the workplace. When leaders reinforce and periodically reward these behaviours, such highly engaged workers remain loyal and productive employees for years.[5] This shared commitment to maintaining trust drives innovation, emancipates talent and enables organizations to outperform their competition.[6]

The seven trust principles required to build our metaphorical well-"trussed" bridge are presented below. As with all supporting structures, the absence of any one weakens the entire entity.

Trust Principle #1: Every successful organization has a shared vision of excellence (SVE).

During his professional hockey career, Dr. Randy Gregg played for two National Hockey League teams – the Edmonton Oilers and the Vancouver Canucks. At the Edmonton Oilers' training camps, the team shared one vision: "Let's win the Stanley Cup Championship." When Randy attended the Vancouver Canucks' training camp, however, the team's goal was "to try and make the play-offs." The Oilers have been in the NHL since 1979-80, appeared in the championship finals seven times and have won five Stanley Cups. The Canucks have been in the NHL since 1970-71, appeared in the finals twice and have never won a championship. Without a shared vision of excellence, a team, company or organization cannot establish priorities, align resources or focus on winning.

The criteria for a shared vision of excellence are few, but important:

1. The SVE is created by the employees themselves.
2. The SVE is concise and memorable.
3. The SVE describes an outcome of excellence *or* a way of working that delivers an excellent outcome.
4. The SVE enables staff to prioritize their workloads.

> *"Visionary companies are so clear about what they stand for and what they are trying to achieve that they simply don't have room for those unwilling or unable to fit their exacting standards."*
>
> *- James C. Collins & Jerry I. Porras*
> *Authors of Built to Last*

Jack Welch, CEO of General Electric from 1981 to 1995, searched for a way to manage the many different businesses that GE operated. He managed the conglomerate by popularizing the following SVE:

> "We are going to be the most competitive enterprise in the world by being No. 1 or No. 2 in every market." [7]

This meant that every GE division, whether it sold jet engines or manufactured household appliances, either led its industry or was the competition. Welch claims the statement came about by listening to smart people throughout the organization.

This message was repeated at every meeting and used as rationale for business decisions. If a GE division failed to meet its target, it was overhauled, sold off or closed. Every new initiative conformed to the SVE, and employees who supported it were publicly rewarded. Those unable to deliver according to the SVE were let go. In the process, GE became the world's largest and most valuable company.

Trust Principle #2: Successful leaders model trust principles.

When Carlos Ghosn helped turn around the giant auto maker Nissan, he did so by modeling the same trust behaviours (in this case personal accountability and following through on commitments) he expected from his staff.

> Right from the beginning I made it clear that every number had to be thoroughly checked. I did not accept any report that was less than totally clear and verifiable, and I expected people to personally commit to every observation or claim they made. I set an example myself. When I announced the revival plan, I also declared that I would resign if we failed to accomplish any of the commitments we set for ourselves.[8]

Another "turnaround" leader, former IBM CEO Louis V. Gerstner Jr., tackled the challenge of changing the culture of corporate giant IBM by instituting another trust principle, clarity of communication:

> The best leaders create high-performance cultures. They set demanding goals, measure results and

hold people accountable... Leadership is about communication, openness and a willingness to speak often and honestly...[9]

Trust Principle #3: Successful organizations abide by a code of conduct that is created by employees, known by all and modeled by leaders.

Codes of conduct used to be the exclusive domain of the military, where strict adherence to rules was necessary to save lives. Now, such codes operate in educational settings, amongst special interest groups, and are commonplace in the corporate world. Prudential, Unilever PLC and GlaxoSmithKline have all developed, abide by and do business with other organizations whose formal codes of conduct guide employee behaviour.[10]

Some might argue that if a team or organization is relatively small and close-knit, there is no need for a written code of conduct, team charter or similar document. Team members and employees already understand the professional standards of behaviour required to perform their jobs, so why take the time and effort to codify these behaviours? The answer lies in the rate of change. A team or organization is rarely static and people leave, are hired and move all the time. Having a written code enables new and recently-transferred employees to understand exactly what is expected of them. It also serves to remind existing staff about the reasons for implementing trust principles, particularly when an individual's cynicism and negativity can begin to affect the entire workplace.

Trust Principle #4: Provide staff context and rationale when assigning tasks.

> "...treat every employee as someone who deserves to know what's going on in the enterprise."
>
> -Lou Gerstner

The adage "Tell me and I will forget; show me and I may remember; involve me and I will understand" applies directly to workplace communication. If managers simply assign tasks without giving context and rationale, employees fail to link their tasks to the bigger picture. Eventually employees forget about the bigger picture, lose interest in their jobs and become disengaged from their work.

When Sears was undergoing massive restructuring in the mid-1990s, it encountered resistance to change throughout the organization. In an effort to understand why, a senior executive visited several of the stores and asked employees how much revenue they thought Sears earned from every dollar of goods sold. Most employees answered "45 cents"; the correct answer was less than one cent. Knowing the razor-thin margins helped sales associates understand the drastic need for change and brought staff onside with the restructuring initiatives.[11]

Trust Principle #5: All workplace communication should have certainty.

There is only one way to communicate that is guaranteed to build trust. It is called "100 percent closure" and it is the brainchild of Arthur Ciancutti and Thomas Steding, co-authors of *Built on Trust: Gaining Competitive Advantage in Any Industry.*

One hundred percent closure is a specific agreement about what will be done by whom and when. Sounds incredibly simple, right? You assign a task to an employee and tell him exactly when it's due. This happens all the time, so what's the big deal?

The big deal is that we rarely communicate with certainty. Our lexicon of workplace phrases is full of ambiguity. Can you get this finished "as soon as possible," "pretty soon," "right away," "later," "possibly next week," etc.? Each of these phrases means something different to everyone and therein is the problem. In the absence of certainty, people assume different things and these assumptions *always* lead to misunderstandings, mistakes, blaming and ill feelings between co-workers. Even worse than ambiguous communication are employees who promise to complete tasks without even thinking about their current workloads or whether or not they are capable of committing to a task. Disengaged employees sometimes make false promises and commitments intentionally, adding to workplace frustration, stress and drama.

Practicing 100 percent closure avoids these traps by eliminating assumptions from the conversation and by making people think about their current tasks before committing to a new one. Here is how it works:

1. Manager A assigns employee B a task.
2. B asks questions about the task while A listens, providing strategic, contextual and relevant information.

3. A and B negotiate time and agree to a firm due date, e.g. Tuesday, November 27th at 2 p.m.
4. If circumstances arise and B is unable to maintain his commitment, he immediately contacts A, making a new agreement for completion.
5. When B completes the assignment, A thanks B and acknowledges B's contribution.

Implementing 100 percent closure requires a disciplined, respectful approach to communication. Employees commit to listen to each other, share information, come to a mutual agreement, leave open the lines of communication and praise one another when agreements are kept. This approach is practiced by the most effective organizations.

"The core competency that precedes and envelops the others [is] listening with the intent to learn and the commitment to act." [12]

Trust Principle #6: Empower teams whenever possible.

In almost every organization, it is possible to harness the energy, commitment and productivity of highly energized people within a functional team. The conditions for teamwork must be present, however, to distinguish a functional, trust-based team – one that operates using trust principles – from a nominal team, a "team" in name only. Being part of a "trust team" is always a rewarding experience.

At a Building Workplace Trust© seminar for managers, one civil servant shared this trust team story:

We were watching the budget debates on TV when our (government) minister announced to the House (the provincial legislature) that the public would be able to pay their taxes on-line by June 14. This was in March and we were shocked by the minister's promise! We had been working on a system, but the application's development was in its very initial stages. Our boss had made a public commitment, however, and he expected us to make it happen on time and on budget.

We gathered the team around, about twenty people from various parts of the ministry. Everyone knew what had to be done and the tight timelines we were under. Right then, everyone gave their personal commitment to getting the system up and running by June 14.

Looking back, I have to say that a number of factors contributed directly to our team being successful. We had the right mix of skills and experience around the table. We were able to share critical information and speak our minds freely; there just wasn't time to be polite or worry about someone's ego. If something wasn't working, you said so right away. No one's feelings got hurt; we just tried to brainstorm another way around the problem.

When we needed additional resources for this or that, we made the request to senior management and they supported it right away. It isn't always like that in bureaucracy, but it was very refreshing to obtain approvals for requests that quickly.

We worked a lot of overtime, put in lots of weekends and had more than a few setbacks. Despite some demanding moments, however, everyone was energized by the project. We even managed to have some fun along the way!

The project was completed on time and on budget. Everyone on the team got a personal letter from the minister thanking us for our hard work. It was very gratifying to get that kind of recognition in an organization of over 4,000 employees.[13]

While functional teams exist in almost any organization, many of the conditions that enable them to succeed are just trust principles in operation. In the civil service example above:

1. people shared a vision that required an outcome of excellence
2. leaders actively modeled trust behaviours by listening to the team's needs and providing team members timely support
3. everyone on the team behaved according to an informal code of conduct, e.g., personally committing to the due date

4. critical information was freely shared with team members, keeping everyone informed of issues and progress
5. members communicated with certainty, evidenced by the way the team gave feedback, contributed solutions and followed through on commitments.

Teams are the incubator for organizational trust. When people participate in functional teams, they (and their organization) experience the many benefits and advantages of a trust-based workplace.

Trust Principle #7: Strategic planning and implementation are best done inclusively.

When it comes time to take a step back from the day-to-day operations of your organization and engage in some strategic planning, it is a good idea to remember the World War I battle of Vimy Ridge.

Vimy Ridge is a seven-kilometre long height of land in northwest France. The German Army captured Vimy in September 1914 and from this strategic vantage point was able to monitor and disrupt Allied troop movements. From September 1914 to April 1917, the Germans reinforced their position with a series of trenches, bunkers, caves, tunnels and concrete gun emplacements. Vimy was so fortified, in fact, that 150,000 French soldiers had been killed and wounded attempting to recapture it.

When the Canadian Army was given the task of taking back Vimy Ridge in 1917, division commanders Byng and Currie were not content to simply throw troops at the heavily reinforced enemy. Instead, they studied the aerial photographs of the German positions provided by Allied pilots. They incorporated tactical suggestions made by machine gunners and artillery troops. They asked engineers for their input. Based on feedback from the various divisions, the Canadians even built a scale model of Vimy Ridge, carefully labelling each enemy position and Canadian objective.

For months prior to the battle, the Canadian troops drilled intensively using the model of Vimy to familiarize themselves with all elements of the upcoming assault. Byng instructed officers "to encourage every soldier to ask questions" so that everyone knew his task. For the first time in the war, every soldier – not just the officers – was given detailed maps of the upcoming battle. "The knowledge that nothing had been overlooked seeped down to the newest private soldier and contributed to the high morale of the Canadian troops...That high morale produced a victory that helped to turn the tide in the war..."[14]

The Canadians captured Vimy Ridge in three days at a cost of approximately 10,000 killed and wounded men. Despite the tragic losses, the Canadian troops were heartened by their stunning victory, bonding together and sharing a sense of identity. Brigadier-General A. E. Ross commented about the battle "...in those few minutes I witnessed the birth of a nation." The Germans suffered losses of about 20,000 troops and the loss of their strategic position hastened their defeat in the war.[15]

The Vimy Ridge victory's management lessons are instructive. When your organization is facing stiff competition, using the collective intelligence of your entire workforce informs decision-making, improves the strategic planning process and often leads to innovation. Keeping everyone informed also encourages participation and ensures a smoother implementation. Along with greater participation comes a collective sense of accomplishment – you might not only beat the competition, but create something significant and lasting in the process.

Implementing these seven trust principles requires you and your co-workers to change some habits, shift focus and perhaps learn some new skills. As Albert Einstein mused, "We cannot solve our problems with the same thinking we used when we created them."[16]

> *I think one great source of our strength was due to the fact that we always fought together, and as we realized through the lessons war had taught us, that our infantry, artillery, engineers, machine guns, etc., could be strengthened, we changed our organization.*
>
> *-General Arthur Currie,*
> *Speech to the Empire Club*
> *Toronto, 1919*

Chapter 2
Changing Organizational Culture

Assuming you recognize the need to change your workplace environment, your first question may be, "Is it really possible to change an organization's culture?"

The answer is "yes" – but it does take time. When I began working at the British Columbia Ministry of Health in 1988, smoking was permitted in the break rooms on floors one, three, five and seven. Imagine that – smoking at the Ministry of Health!

It wasn't simply that people were permitted to smoke cigarettes; their habits and behaviour affected the culture of the organization. People arranged their meeting times based on their need to smoke periodically throughout the work day. Because they shared break rooms, smokers usually socialized with other smokers. Second-hand smoke permeated throughout the poorly ventilated building, causing high rates of sickness and absenteeism. At one time, you were even allowed to smoke at your desk but were not permitted to talk with your co-workers!

Today, such a situation seems ludicrous. Smoking is banned from all public buildings, in virtually all workplaces, and is permitted only outdoors or in very restricted areas. Did this dramatic change make sense?

Or course it did. It makes sense to protect people from the noxious fumes of cigarettes. It makes perfect sense to prevent or restrict those behaviours that used to be tolerated but are now proven to create a toxic working environment. Just as smoking is no longer permissible in the workplace, so too is it time to ban other unhealthy habits – dishonesty, gossiping, favouritism, bullying, etc. All of these behaviours (and others) occur in organizations, creating toxic environments that feed workplace stress. Does it make sense to ban such behaviours? Of course it does.

It took a few years for the Health Ministry to rid itself completely of smoking and the negative behaviours it propagated. The changes were sweeping and forced people to adopt new, healthier habits or be seriously inconvenienced. The organization completely changed this aspect of its culture, and its employees were healthier and more productive for it.

The same holds true for changing the culture of an organization with dysfunctional management practices and unengaged employees. It is a matter of banning "unhealthy" habits and instituting practices that reward positive, productive and trustful behaviours.

When Jack Welch took over as the CEO of corporate giant General Electric, he found an organizational culture steeped in "bureaucracy, layers politicking and false politeness." People were afraid to speak their minds, share information or express doubt. Fear, complacency and inertia characterized GE's culture.

To make GE a world leader, Welch needed to change all that. He knew the organizational culture was stifling smart ideas and holding people back from contributing their best. To encourage employees to speak up and be honest with one another, Welch became very outspoken at meetings, encouraging staff to follow his example and speak with "candour." At first, the approach shocked people, but Welch systematically introduced change to the old habits.

"To get candour, you reward it, praise it and talk about it. Most of all, you yourself demonstrate it in an exuberant and even exaggerated way."[17] Welch lists "candour" as one of the most important influences he brought to GE.

Can organizational culture be changed for the better? The answer is demonstrably "yes." Before that happens, however, leaders have to acknowledge that significant changes are necessary and that organizational culture needs to evolve.

Perhaps the next chapter will convince you that drastic changes are needed now.

Chapter 3
Problems in the Workplace

While trust exists in small pockets within every organization, it is a scarce commodity that very few employees experience regularly. One only has to look at recent employment engagement scores in North America to realize that most people do not experience enough trust to enable them to bring their best efforts to work. One in five workers is considered "highly engaged" and willingly gives more effort than is required. Three of every five North American employees are "moderately engaged," performing the minimum amount of work required to fulfill their duties and responsibilities. The remaining employees are "disengaged" – staff who under-perform and sometimes disrupt the productive work of others.

> *"Our research underscores that an effective employment proposition goes well beyond pay and benefits..."*
>
> *- Excerpt from Towers Perrin Study*

A 2005 Towers Perrin Global Workforce Study[18] yielded the following engagement scores for North American workers:

Country	% highly engaged	% moderately engaged	% disengaged
United States	21%	63%	16%
Canada	17%	66%	17%

Look around your workplace – eighty percent of the people in your organization are not bringing their best efforts to work. Just think of the lost productivity and waste of talent!

And it gets worse. Consider these workplace facts:

- Job related stress costs American industry an estimated $300 billion a year, *more than the net profits of all the Fortune 500 companies combined.*
- Over fifty percent of the 550 million working days lost each year in the USA because of absenteeism are due to stress.
- A 2003 survey of over 31,000 Canadian workers found more than half felt stressed, one-third felt depressed, twenty-five percent thought of quitting their jobs at least once a week or more and ten percent reported high absenteeism due to emotional, physical or mental fatigue.
- According to one recent survey finding, fifty percent of Baby Boomers have effectively retired on the job.
- Typical managers work fifty-one hours per week; with a Blackberry, this number increases to seventy-one hours per week.[19]
- In a 2004 survey, eighty-four percent of executives from large corporations admitted they did not take advantage of their workforce's full potential.[20]
- A 2005 Ipsos Reid survey found that fifty-three percent of CEOs and fifty-two percent of employees agree that their organizations are not as productive as they should be, citing stress, burnout and mental health issues as the top reasons negatively affecting productivity.[21]

We are working longer hours and experiencing greater stress. Our productivity is lagging and yet we are unable to fulfill our potential!

As if these disturbing trends aren't enough, consider how the accelerating rate of technological change is transforming our workplace. Twenty years ago, office staff hand-wrote correspondence for a secretary who typed copies using carbon paper. There was one slow fax machine requiring special paper. There was no e-mail, Microsoft Office or PDA. Primitive word processors began appearing on desks only in the late 1980s.

Less than a generation ago, we did the tasks set out in our job descriptions, received information via office memos and worked at a comfortable pace. Concepts like telecommuting, "virtual" offices or "on-line" collaboration were unheard of. Greater numbers of female managers and more diverse workforces began to impact organizational practices, while environmental and ethical considerations were absorbed gradually into the corporate consciousness.[22] We were just getting our minds around the concepts of global competition, the end of the USSR and the dramatic rise of the Asian economies.

Fast forward twenty years. Along with our PCs and laptops, Blackberries connect us to virtual offices anywhere, anytime. Huge amounts of data are sent and received across continents at the speed of light. Every morning we scan dozens of e-mails, voice mails and pod casts just to stay informed. We perform a wide variety of tasks – so much so that we sometimes lose focus. And the tasks bear little resemblance to our original job descriptions.[23] Most of us take work home – on PDA, jump drives, laptops, in briefcases and certainly in our minds. The workplace hours are 24/7, the workforce has greater diversity and ethical and environmental considerations dictate our agenda.

For all of these revolutionary changes, however, organizational structures have not evolved to keep pace. At the top is a CEO, president or deputy minister, supported by an executive or management committee, middle managers, supervisors and employees. Organizations are divided into functional departments – finance, operations, sales, information technology, communications, human resources, sales, etc. – each with its own chain of command.[24] The generic job titles that are reflected on an organizational chart – vice president, general manager, director, executive assistant, etc. – reveal the hierarchies and bureaucracies designed to serve the organization's mission, corporate policies and procedures, regulations, protocols and various systems. The accountability is to the marketplace, shareholders, owners, the public, politicians, regulatory bodies, employees and ultimately the judicial system. Despite incredible technological change, corporate structures have remained near constant for decades.[25]

Nor have staffing or communication practices experienced many changes. Most employees are hired based on their ability to demonstrate a skill or aptitude.[26] Each employee has a job description of tasks, duties and responsibilities. Many people are promoted not because they possess leadership qualities, but due to the Peter Principle, favouritism, seniority, technical proficiency or other irrelevant factors. Electronic communications like the internet, intranet and e-mail have replaced the memo, yet important information still flows from the top down with the inherent risks of miscommunication and misinterpretation.

Several initiatives have tried to cope with the dramatic changes, addressing issues associated with lagging productivity and technical change. Some included efforts to improve organizational performance by re-focusing managers. Others tried to enhance quality and increase productivity by improving the communications skills of leaders and teams. You may remember some of these concepts finding their way into your organization – Management by Objective, Total Quality Management (TQM), Process Re-engineering, 360 Feedback and Personality Profiling, etc. When organizational thinkers and academics measured the effectiveness of some of these approaches, however, the results were discouraging – ninety percent of TQM initiatives failed; seventy percent of process re-engineering projects failed;[27] and as for the ability of 360 Feedback and Personality Profiling exercises to improve team functioning, there are no known successes.[28]

Even educational attempts to cope with these dramatic changes have had mixed results. Despite the incredible advances in information and communication technologies, our personal communication skills are declining.[29] Rapidly-changing technologies mean that we continually face a steep learning curve. Organizations have responded by spending *less* money on training, learning and development than they did ten years ago.[30] Instances of workplace bullying have increased, as have the disturbing number of incidences in workplace violence.[31] As if to underline these challenges, new phrases have entered into our lexicon about dealing with "role overload" and trying to achieve a "work/life balance."[32]

These are not the signs of a healthy, productive labour force. They are the signs of working people struggling to cope. These employees – your employees – need a different work environment if your organization is going to continue functioning into the next decade. They need lasting, positive changes to their workplace to enable them to grow and fulfill their potential. Management guru Peter F. Drucker makes the point succinctly:

> A business enterprise (or any other institution) has only one true resource: people. It succeeds by making human resources productive.[33]

Business leaders have long acknowledged the challenge of motivating the majority of employees. Jack Welch encouraged managers to concentrate on this "middle seventy percent," the bulk of employees "who don't quite shine but who work hard and well." Welch instructed his managers to "fight gravity, and instead of taking the middle seventy per cent for granted, treat them like the heart and soul of the organization." [34]

Building a trust culture targets the middle seventy percent by supporting behaviours that encourage participation, improve corporate communication and reduce workplace stress. The next chapter describes how a few changes can dramatically affect the way you and your employees feel about going to work.

Chapter 4
The Trust Organization

Leaving behind the current problems of the workplace for a moment, imagine yourself on your daily commute. Instead of stressing about the demands of the upcoming week, you feel excited about its prospects. Rather than dreading having to deal with certain staff, you are looking forward to interacting with your colleagues. Instead of being anxious and tired, you feel energized, confident in your abilities to contribute and proud of the work that you and your co-workers do.

Imagine that every person in your organization feels the same way and experiences the same positive energy.

Imagine that every employee knows exactly what tasks to accomplish in the next six months. When challenges and barriers to progress do arise, co-workers enthusiastically brainstorm together to determine effective alternatives.

Imagine that everyone in your organization communicates with certainty and purpose.

Imagine that your organization encourages you to do your job, your way.

Finally, imagine that everyone in your organization follows through on his or her commitments, treats each other respectfully and that senior managers lead by example.

Does this describe your current workplace experience and your organization? Probably not.

> *"...Toyota's philosophy of mutual trust between team members and the company [is] the only route to mutual prosperity and progress."*
>
> *-excerpt from www.toyota.ca*

With a few small changes, however, it could.

Becoming a trust organization does not require a significant outlay of resources or a re-structuring of your business. It does mean, however, that certain behaviours must be entrenched and others completely eliminated. It means that trust practices – leading by example, following through on commitments, refusing to participate in gossip, etc. – must be adopted by everyone, modeled by senior managers and positively reinforced at every opportunity. [35]

Based on our research and experience, we believe that the vast majority of employees in your organization, whether enthusiastic new hires or long-term employees, are looking for opportunities to contribute their talents, skills and experience. Everyone wants to feel that he or she is contributing and making progress; therefore, the potential to build trust exists within every employee.

It will take a while for these "new" behaviours to become standard practice. Once they take root and define the organization's culture, however, it becomes "the way we do things around here." An organization with a positive culture and reputation for success has little trouble retaining experienced staff or attracting and acculturating bright new employees.

The business case for building trust in an organization is compelling – way beyond lowering retention and recruitment costs. Indeed, many books and magazine articles have been written on the benefits of having trustful relationships dominate an organizational culture.[36] The bottom line is that a workplace culture based on trust creates efficiencies within an organization that enable it to be more competitive, profitable and well-respected. Companies like WestJet, Toyota [37] and eBay[38] have already discovered this fact.

The next few chapters explain exactly how this is accomplished, what is required to build trust and what to do when certain obstacles to trust arise. Before we proceed to our explanation, however, let's look at a real "trust" organization and compare it to an amalgam of familiar, average organizations.

Chapter 5
Trust Organization vs. the Average Organization

How does a trust organization compare to an average one?

Table 1
Trust Organization vs. Average Organization

Trust Organization	Average Organization[39]
Senior managers act with transparency, know everyone, lead by example.	Senior management is perceived as aloof, self-interested.
Every employee knows what the organization does and why. This "common vision" comes from the staff itself–employees refer to it frequently and proudly.	There is a mission statement that no one can quote. There is no common vision or unifying theme.
Managers encourage staff to use their own judgment.	Employees perceive a lack of information to do their jobs to the best of their ability.
Communication is based on the principle of 100 percent closure. Information is freely shared; giving context, rationale & strategic info is the norm.	Most employees cite a lack of communication as the main reason for distrust and underperformance; managers are perceived as hoarding information.
Commitments are kept, teams are used, staff volunteer for tasks.	People do not always follow through on commitments; workloads are uneven.

A Trust Organization

WestJet, Canada's discount airline is an excellent example of a trust organization. It begins with leaders who demonstrate the very organizational values they expect from employees. In 2003, WestJet CEO Clive Beddoes flew to England to give a speech at the Canadian Club in London. Beddoes showed up at the exclusive club only moments before his presentation. He explained his lateness by relating that while he was at the airport, he met with WestJet staff to share the corporate strategy and some new initiatives with them. He then took additional time to answer employees' questions and engage them in a full and productive discussion.[40]

By taking the time to share WestJet's vision and *listen* to staff feedback, CEO Beddoes models several important trust behaviours. First, he considers it a priority that all staff – even those farthest away from corporate headquarters – are informed of new corporate initiatives and made to feel part of the team. Secondly, he ensures employees have an opportunity to share their feedback with him, demonstrating respect for their contributions. Thirdly, he models the level of commitment he expects from others – enthusiastically discussing WestJet business after an eight and a half hour flight and before an important presentation.

> *"Beddoe's actions show with that he cares about the employees. The employees, sensing that he is sincere, care about Beddoes and the organization; they "reward" his behaviour with engagement.[41]*

Not surprisingly, such leadership energizes and encourages staff. In fact, WestJet workers refer to themselves as "WestJetters," not simply as "employees." This common identity is linked to the common vision of WestJetters – "to think like owners."[42] This shared vision also encourages initiative. WestJetters are challenged to find innovative ways to enhance productivity and to deliver consistently higher levels of customer service. The message is effective in reinforcing productive behaviours. WestJet operates with seventy-five staff per plane; rival Air Canada needs 135 employees to operate the same plane.[43]

WestJetters are hired based on their positive attitudes, then trained on the job to acquire the necessary skills. Working within an environment stressing teamwork and accountability, employees are encouraged to problem-solve using their own talents and burgeoning judgment. Management sets goals, not directives, has guidelines as opposed to rigid procedures and makes promises rather than quoting policies. This flexible approach allows staff to develop their own judgment and abilities consistent with the organization's well-known vision.

While leaders give staff discretion to pursue great customer service, the senior management team also models the personal accountability that promotes "thinking like an owner." When the company wasn't profitable for a time during 2006, CEO Clive Beddoes took personal responsibility for failing to predict raising fuel prices and slashed his salary to $1. Two years earlier, Beddoes offered his resignation to the board over a lawsuit launched by rival Air Canada in which a former WestJet executive was implicated in corporate espionage activities.

"Clearly I have to take responsibility...and no individual, including myself, should have the latitude to act irresponsibly."[44] Other senior managers exemplified this code of personal accountability and the commitment to customer service. WestJet co-founder and pilot Donald Bell regularly flew round trips to gain firsthand feedback from staff and customers as a means to check corporate performance. It isn't unusual for employees to see members of the senior management team cleaning the airplanes between flights!

As a further indication of the level of corporate trust (and in stark contrast to the rest of the airline industry), there are no unions at WestJet. Instead, WestJetters fund a Pro-active Communications Team (PACT) to represent their concerns to the company. Formal channels of corporate communication are augmented by internal newsletters and by holding staff parties frequently to celebrate organizational successes.

In an industry where ninety-seven percent of start-ups fail, WestJet was profitable after four months in operation. Since 1996 it has grown from three airplanes and 220 employees to sixty-three airplanes and over 6,000 employees. From 2002 to 2007, revenues grew from $683 million to $1.8 billion. WestJet's new goal is to be among the top twenty airlines in the world by 2015. The company attributes much of this success to its "positive corporate culture." It is a corporate culture based largely upon trust.

The success of an organization like WestJet demonstrates the superior approach of trust-based organizations. Unless you have spent your entire career with a trust-based organization, however, it is more likely that you have experienced the culture of the average organization, as described below.

An Average Organization

An average organization shares a number of characteristics that form its culture and determine its level of performance. One of the most striking characteristics is that most employees lack confidence in their leadership. Even when a majority of employees enjoy positive working relationships with their supervisors, few feel the same way about the senior executives.

In 2006, employee engagement surveys were conducted by two large Canadian civil services. Almost seventy-five percent of staff indicated a "positive relationship" with their immediate supervisor and believed their supervisors "cared about them as people." Fewer than half of employees (forty-three percent) had confidence in their organizational leaders and only thirty-three percent believed senior managers were interested in their well-being, did a good job of employee recognition or provided clear direction.[45]

Many CEOs do not make corporate communication a priority, losing valuable opportunities to connect with staff. A recent survey of 100 corporate communication professionals found that only ten percent believed their organization's executive could effectively deliver corporate messages.[46] Add to this the employees' perception that senior managers simply do not value their contribution to the organization. In a recent global survey of 90,000 workers, only ten percent believed that senior management treated them as if they were the organization's most important resource.[47]

The perception of greed and lack of accountability of some high profile CEOs has also undermined employee confidence. In 1980, a CEO was paid forty-two times the wages of an average employee. By 2005, CEO compensation was 411 times the amount paid to an average employee. If pay was linked to performance, this astounding pay raise would be understandable and perhaps justified.[48] In many instances, however, organizational leaders have received raises and bonuses even as their organization underperformed or suffered losses. For example, former Home Deport CEO Robert Nardelli received US$200 million in compensation while his company's stock price remained unchanged during his five years of leadership.[49]

This inability of leaders to connect with employees is often reflected in the bland, uninspiring mission statements of most average organizations. All too frequently, mission statements are imposed on organizations from distant corporate headquarters instead of being organically inspired and grown from within. At our Building Workplace Trust Management Seminars©, we often ask if anyone in the audience can quote for us their organization's mission statement. So far, no one has been able to do so. The purpose of this exercise is not to embarrass anyone but to demonstrate that a mission statement should arise from within, be known by all and should serve to guide employees. Without a common and frequently communicated vision, how do workers prioritize tasks or focus on strategic initiatives?

Perhaps the most limiting practice in average organizations is that leaders and mangers fail to pass on strategic information to employees. Instead of explaining an assignment's context and rationale, supervisors simply assign employees tasks and expect them to carry them out. When employees are told to do something but aren't told why, they eventually stop wondering why. Experienced employees eventually limit their efforts to fulfilling the task at hand, failing to use their knowledge to add value to the organization or to link their duties to organizational goals. Based on surveys of 50,000 employees in seventy organizations, about half say they do not receive enough information to perform their jobs well.[50] The result is missed opportunities for improved outcomes, innovation and collaboration.

Average organizations typically have departments that operate independently of each other. The lack of interdepartmental communication, also known as "siloing," invariably leads to poor decision-making and bungled projects. As Tom Peters wrote twenty years ago, "Rip apart a badly developed project and you will unfailingly find seventy-five percent of the slippage attributable to 'siloing,' or sending memos and minutes up and down vertical organizational 'silos' or 'stove pipes' for decisions..."[51]

This classic pattern of isolated communication is common in organizations with rigid policies, procedures and bureaucracies. It has been attributed to such blunders as the Bush administration's mishandling of intelligence information prior to the invasion of Iraq[52] and the Challenger Space Shuttle disaster.[53]

There is also a growing tendency for senior managers to avoid accepting responsibility for their actions. Spectacular recent corporate scandals like WorldCom, Enron, Hollinger, the Royal Canadian Mounted Police and the successful prosecutions of Bernard Ebbers, Kenneth Lay, Conrad Black and many other high profile executives demonstrate an astounding lack of conscience and personal accountability. The recent growth of laws, policies and entire associations to protect organizational "whistleblowers" further testifies to this lamentable trend.

If the poor communication practices of average organizations often begin in the corner office, they are compounded by departmental "stove pipes" and do their most damage in the hands of front-line managers and supervisors. Formal employee recognition programs are a poor substitute for managers who consistently miss opportunities to praise the extraordinary day-to-day efforts of employees. Employee "renewal initiatives" – communicated in fragmented messages lacking sincerity – are greeted by staff with cynicism and negativity.[54] Managers who consistently hoard information frustrate staff and limit their potential to contribute. Over time, employees who feel "out of the loop" adopt a more negative view of their leaders and of their organization. People simply lose trust in their leaders, their organization and eventually, in themselves.

The presence or absence of trust has a profound effect upon workforce motivation, engagement and productivity. In a trust organization, employees feel confident and energized enough to give extraordinary efforts and produce excellent results *on a regular basis*. In an average organization, however, the majority of people do not feel engaged or particularly motivated. The absence of trust prevents them from bringing all their efforts to benefit the organization.

Chapter 6
The "Feel" of Trust

What does workplace trust feel like?

Many of us have had the rewarding experience of being part of a highly productive workplace team. The team contained just the right mixture of skilled people, leadership, accountability and drive. We were able to accomplish incredible things under tight deadlines. We worked hard, respected each other's abilities, communicated effectively and found time to have a little fun. The work was important, our accomplishments were sincerely acknowledged and each member felt exhilarated at the opportunity to contribute his or her own unique talents. The excitement of contributing combined with the camaraderie of energized colleagues is what workplace trust looks and feels like.

Perhaps you have also worked for organizations where little trust existed. Fear prevented you (and others) from speaking up at staff meetings and voicing honest opinions. Favouritism, not competency, seemed to determine training opportunities and promotions. Rumours, gossip and negative assumptions about co-workers abounded; accurate, instructive and contextual communication was scarce.

In such fear-based work environments, instead of being excited and motivated, you felt emotionally exhausted, barely able to get through the day. Perhaps you even dreaded going to work and channelled your energies into outside activities or even into finding a new job! In workplaces where the desire to contribute was quashed, it is the unsuccessful search for trust that eventually frustrates and extinguishes motivation and potential. There is no sense of team or team spirit. Consequently, employees feel isolated and often frustrated at not being able to contribute their talents. Eventually, they stop trying to contribute altogether.

The majority of us likely work at organizations that fall somewhere between the two extremes. Occasionally, we may be motivated by an opportunity to work on a potentially interesting project that allows us to demonstrate our skills and abilities. Most of the time, however, we are conditioned to perform our jobs as the circumstances allow. Our professionalism, motivation and performance vary depending upon how we perceive our value to the organization and the integrity of our leaders. If we sense the organization is less than 100 percent committed to us, we bring less than 100 percent of our commitment to work. We vacillate between excitement and frustration, reflected in our varying performance and level of commitment to our organization.

Let's look at the following real-life examples of Alan, Brenda and Carl to see how trust operates on an individual level.

Alan

Alan needs his boss's approval to implement a new system. The proposal is to develop an on-line manual for regional managers who need temporary, contracted services to meet operational requirements. Alan came up with the idea after reviewing contracts from three regional managers, two of whom dramatically overspent while purchasing the same services.

Alan has put a lot of time and effort into the proposal and believes that it could save the organization a substantial amount of money by streamlining administrative practices and rationalizing costs.
As he pitches his idea to the boss, Alan is hoping for specific feedback. "Will the boss like my idea? Will he see that I have worked hard on this? Will he enable me to try this out and really see if the idea makes good business sense for the organization?" In short, Alan is looking for an opportunity to demonstrate his talent and earn trust.

Alan's boss listens attentively to the proposal, praising him for his initiative. He gives Alan specific feedback concerning the proposal, including constructive criticism and some strategic information. He tells Alan that the organization is looking to set policy guidelines for contracting services and provides Alan with minutes from a recent management meeting concerning this very issue. They set a timetable for revising the proposal and a mutually-agreed upon meeting date and time to review progress.

Alan leaves the meeting feeling appreciated and believing that he is contributing to the organization. His gut instinct was right; there are savings to be made by streamlining the contracting process. The boss acknowledged Alan's hard work and provided him with valuable feedback to enable Alan to move forward with his potential project. Alan feels good about using his talents and initiative to add value to the organization; Alan's boss is helping him contribute by encouraging his efforts, sharing vital information and positively reinforcing Alan's initiative.

Alan and his boss are developing a trust relationship. Alan feels he was given a legitimate opportunity to demonstrate his unique skills to the organization; his boss facilitated that opportunity for Alan; the organization benefits by utilizing the talents of its employees. *Even if the proposal never gets implemented,* the trust between Alan and his boss is developing. If their behaviour remains consistent, it will define their productive relationship for years.

The opportunity for Alan to earn trust, made possible by his boss's interest and encouragement, benefits the organization by realizing savings through the initiative or by using resources to their full potential. Everyone wins: the employee, the manager and the organization.

Brenda

Brenda, a workflow re-design specialist, was recently hired by a large communications firm. Brenda was enthusiastic about wanting to make an immediate contribution to her new work unit. She noticed that the workflow in her department was inconsistent – redundant work processes caused uneven workloads and some staff ended up doing a lot more work than others. At a staff meeting, Brenda offered a few suggestions for improving workflow, volunteering to establish and chair the department's workflow re-design committee.

No one seemed particularly interested in Brenda's ideas or in her willingness to do committee work. Her supervisor was outwardly perturbed at Brenda's suggestions, and assigned Brenda lots of additional work. Brenda feels she is almost being punished for trying to make the office more productive. She perceives that she is making little progress and that no one is particularly interested in her suggestions, extra efforts or in the findings of the workflow re-design committee.

After a few months, Brenda is frustrated by a perception of indifference to her work and the lack of positive feedback. She starts looking for other places in the organization where she can possibly contribute her skills and talents; searching for people who may be receptive to her suggestions and ideas. She doesn't seem to find any managers who value her experience and begins to wonder if the firm is a good fit for her. Brenda's enthusiasm wanes and instead of bringing 100 percent of her effort to work every day, she eventually manages to bring seventy percent, then sixty percent, and so on.

The people in Brenda's organization also perceive her frustration and inconsistent effort. She receives uneven employee appraisals and some label her a "troublemaker." It is an unhealthy situation. Believing there is insufficient support to enable her to progress, Brenda becomes a "moderately engaged" employee; she puts in just enough effort to perform the minimum requirements of her job. She leaves the firm after eighteen months, finding a better-paying job with a similar organization. The firm now has to replace Brenda, at an estimated cost of 100 to 150 percent of her annual salary.[55] No one wins. Brenda did not fulfill her potential, the firm did not benefit from her talents and the cost of replacing her negatively impacts the organization as a whole.

Carl

Carl's organization is young, aggressive and full of opportunities - just like Carl! A recent MBA grad, Carl was very enthusiastic when he got his job as a management consultant with a medium-sized, human resources consulting company. He often stayed late, producing financial reports, learning the business and putting in a lot of extra effort. Carl's boss noticed his enthusiasm and willingness to learn and eventually gave Carl full responsibility for ensuring the division's profitability. After the first fiscal year, Carl's boss was pleased with the bottom line results and told clients that Carl would someday take over the firm!

At a senior management meeting a few weeks later, however, the boss took credit for all of Carl's work. Carl was shocked and felt his trust had been betrayed. To his mind, he'd worked hard to earn trust, and until this moment, he had willingly trusted his boss and organization. Carl was shocked and angered by this betrayal and confronted his boss. His boss didn't deny the betrayal and threatened Carl with dismissal. Feeling that he had little to lose, Carl went right to the company president to tell him what had happened. The president listened politely and said that there was really nothing that he could do.

Carl felt that the organization's senior management had *let* the betrayal happen or at the very least, had done nothing to discourage it. Carl was very unhappy; he didn't want to work for an organization that he couldn't trust, and he let everyone in the office know about it. Carl became actively disengaged in his job, disrupting the work of others. By mutual agreement, Carl soon left the organization, eventually founding his own successful company.

The above scenarios – all based on real-life experiences – illustrate how powerful the perception of trust is to motivating or discouraging employees.

Research Findings

Findings based on extensive studies are consistent with the above examples.[56] For example, one team of researchers found that motivation is limited not only by employees' fears, but by a combination of a person's emotional and logical response to a given situation. When an event happens at work, people react both emotionally and intellectually. It is this combination of thoughts and emotions that determine a worker's motivation and productivity.

For instance, the supervisor calls a staff meeting to talk about a new initiative that the company is implementing. Customer service representatives will now begin selling related products and services instead of just handling routine product inquiries. The analytical side of an employee's brain tries to assess the potential of this event. "Is this an opportunity to earn extra income? By supporting this, will I be able to demonstrate my sales ability and perhaps secure a future promotion?" At the staff meeting, employees watch and listen for important cues to enable them to take the most appropriate course of action in relation to the new sales initiative. They are analyzing, reasoning, trying to figure out the best response to boost their standing in the organization.

While one side of the employee's brain assesses the situation and determines the logical response, the other side is formulating an emotional reaction to the same information. This reaction could range from excitement ("What a great idea – how can I get involved?") to cynicism ("Here we go again...") to anger ("I don't believe it! When they hired me they promised I wouldn't have to do sales calls!")

According to the latest research, *both* the logical and emotional reactions determine an employee's level of motivation.

Or is it....Trust?

One might also argue, however, that it is the employee's underlying perception of organizational trust that ultimately influences these "logical" and "emotional" responses. If an employee believes the cross-selling initiative is an opportunity to increase sales and raise his profile in the organization, his enthusiastic reaction is also based on the belief that he trusts his organization to recognize, value and reward his added contribution. If the employee is upset because of a perceived broken promise, however, he might react negatively and try to sabotage the initiative. It is the perception of trust (or mistrust) that ultimately determines his motivation for - and level of participation in - the cross-selling initiative.

Another group of management thinkers agrees with the "underlying trust" explanation. They liken the presence of organizational trust to a diving board: People will jump off the board and commit themselves whole-heartedly to an organization if they believe sufficient trust exists to support them. They will refuse to "jump" and commit themselves, however, if they fear the consequences or if past experiences have demonstrated a pattern of retribution and betrayal.

These management thinkers - Drs. Arky Ciancuitti and Thomas Steding - believe that it is possible to build trust in any organization because the vast majority of people are very motivated and bring to their workplace two basic attributes:

1. the desire to contribute their talents and
2. a belief that their job makes the world a better place.

What prevents these employees from always contributing their best is the emotion of fear – fear of failure, retribution, embarrassment or rejection.[57] Fear dominates the culture of many bureaucracies, large corporations, NGOs and small businesses alike. Every employee wants to contribute his talents and skills but it is the *perception of trust* that tips the scale from fear to contributing. People will overcome their fears when trust principles are evident – for instance, when they see trust behaviours being modeled by senior managers. With trust practices and rules in place, employees feel comfortable enough to speak up and contribute their talents.

There is another, simpler reason why employees respond so well to trust organizations: A trust organization gives them exactly what they want. A 2006 Gallup Poll listed the top four things workers desire from their jobs:

1. the opportunity to use their unique talents and abilities to perform their jobs
2. the chance to interact with others (teamwork) and to help people
3. more flexibility to do the job their way, and
4. flexible working arrangements to provide a better life/work balance.

Consider the first three points – what employees want most is the opportunity to use their skills and talent, work with others and use their own judgment. Sound familiar? Of course it does – organizations like WestJet who hire for these attributes and encourage employees to earn these "desirable" work opportunities reap the reward of highly engaged, highly functional employees.

In average organizations, however, employees face a number of barriers to trust. Whether it is employers not giving employees what they most want, or the "fear stifles contribution" analysis, or the fact that we are complex creatures seeking proof of trust before committing ourselves, the reality is painfully clear: Few organizations provide an environment where the majority of employees can reach their potential, and we should not be surprised that only one in five workers is "highly engaged."[58]

Chapter 7
The Good News:
Workplace Trust Already Exists

The first step toward building trust in any organization is to remind employees that trust already exists in their workplace. Not only does it exist, but many staff have fully participated in trust behaviours and benefited from the experience. Really? How? When?

To answers these questions, conduct this simple experiment. Call a staff meeting and ask employees this question:

"What is the best team you were ever on at work?"

Break the large number up into smaller groups, provide some flip charts and ask them to write down all the characteristics that made their team the "best." At this point, you will observe that people become very animated when describing their enjoyable experiences, great teammates, collective accomplishments and the fun they had being part of a productive group. In less than thirty minutes, lists of characteristics will appear, looking something like this:

CHARACTERISTICS OF MY BEST WORKPLACE TEAM

- HAD A CLEAR GOAL AND DEADLINE
- FOCUSED
- POSSESSED A SHARED BELIEF OR VISION
- EVERYONE FOLLOWED THROUGH ON COMMITMENTS
- MEMBERS FELT EMPOWERED

- RESPECT FOR MEMBERS' ABILITIES AND STRENGTHS
- RECOGNITION FOR ACCOMPLISHMENTS
- LEADERSHIP PROVIDED ENCOURAGEMENT
- MEMBERS COMMUNICATED WITH OPENNESS AND RESPECT
- ALL MEMBERS WERE COMPETENT
- CONSTRUCTIVE CRITICISM, POSITIVE CRITICISM
- LOTS OF PERSONAL AND SOCIAL CONTACT
- OPPORTUNITIES TO PARTICIPATE AND CONTRIBUTE
- RESPECT AND RECOGNITION
- INPUT WAS VALUED AND IMPLEMENTED
- LESS PHONE AND E-MAIL COMMUNICATION, MORE FACE-TO-FACE COMMUNICATION TO CAPTURE CREATIVE ENERGY
- CLEAR EXPECTATIONS OF ROLES AND RESPONSIBILITIES
- STRONG LEADERSHIP/SUPPORT BOTH BEHIND-THE-SCENES AND FOR RESOURCES
- TRANSPARENCY
- HAD OWNERSHIP AND RESPONSIBILITY
- VOLUNTEERS SHARED WORKLOADS
- NOT CRISIS-DRIVEN
- LEFT EGOS AT THE DOOR – JUST GOT THE JOB DONE!
- HAD FUN
- OPENNESS FOR DISCUSSION
- RESPECTED OTHERS
- MENTORING
- UNDERSTANDING PERSONALITIES
- WENT FOR LUNCH & OTHER OUTSIDE ACTIVITIES AFTER HOURS
- POSITIVE THINKING
- **LAUGHTER**
- FLEXIBILITY, YET DEPENDENT UPON EACH OTHER
- DIDN'T PLACE BLAME

- DEALT WITH A PROBLEM ONE-ON-ONE – DIDN"T GOSSIP
- CELEBRATED MILESTONES AND VICTORIES
- PERKS AND INCENTIVES, COOPERATION
- SHARED GOALS
- SHARED VISION – KNEW WHEN NEW PLAN WAS NEEDED
- COMPLIMENTED EACH OTHER
- CONFIDENTIALITY
- "YOU DID A GOOD JOB…"
- HELD MEETINGS TO WORK OUT PROBLEMS
- MANAGER ALLOWED STAFF TO MANAGE THEMSELVES
- FUN, FAMILY FROM DAY 1
- HARD WORKERS
- ABLE TO RELY ON EACH OTHER
- ORGANIZED
- VERY STRONG VISION SUPPORTED BY OTHERS
- NO MICRO-MANAGEMENT
- INDEPENDENCE
- **ONE GOAL**
- ALL WORKED TOGETHER IN TIMES OF CRISIS
- WHEN YOU ARE WORKING IN A "WORKABLE TEAM," YOU FEEL IT, YOU KNOW IT
- NEED A GOOD MIX OF PERSONALITIES AND KNOWLEDGE
- NO BACKSTABBING, NO BLAME, CONFIRMATION FOR A GOOD JOB
- DID NOT LET PERSONAL OPINIONS AFFECT WORKING RELATIONSHIPS
- HUMOUR, ABILITY TO LAUGH AT ONESELF
- SHARING & ACCEPTING KNOWLEDGE
- EVERYONE KNEW THEIR RESPONSIBILITY FOR THEIR JOBS
- POSITIVE PRAISE
- TOLERANCE + CARING + RESPECT

- WERE AWARE WHEN A CO-WORKER NEEDED A HELPING HAND
- OWNED UP TO ERRORS
- HONESTY & DIPLOMACY
- FELT FREE TO TALK
- MUTUAL RESPECT
- COMPASSION AND UNDERSTANDING
- RIGHT PERSON/RIGHT JOB
- OPEN MINDED
- THOUGHT OUTSIDE THE BOX
- PROPER TRAINING
- ASKED FOR HELP

With few exceptions, these lists always contain the same few themes:

1. a clear, shared vision of the work to be done
2. an emphasis on individual responsibility and collective accountability
3. respectful and unambiguous communication amongst team members and with team leaders
4. earned recognition
5. supportive leadership
6. having the right mixture of skills and personalities on the team
7. accomplishing a lot within a short time frame and
8. having fun while accomplishing the desired outcome!

The vast majority of people enjoy being on highly functional teams. They relish the camaraderie of colleagues and the chance to contribute their individual skills. Employees relax in the egalitarian atmosphere of team membership and get energized from being in constant communication with co-workers. They thrive on being accountable for a final product and having the opportunity to apply their talents, knowledge and experience to get the job done properly.

Teams take justifiable pride in their collective accomplishments, particularly when these efforts are recognized by colleagues, senior managers and customers. Without exception, people on effective work teams experience the "highs" of contributing, learning, progressing and of making a positive difference through their organization.

Why then wouldn't every organization in the world want to exploit the effectiveness and productivity of teamwork?

Well, they do. Forty per cent of Fortune 100 companies claim that that "teamwork" is a core value. Nearly every large organization speaks in glowing terms about the value of "teamwork" and wanting to encourage the "pooling of talents and energy."[59] Only a few organizations, however, are consistently able to establish the conditions that allow teams – and trust – to thrive.

Five Conditions

The conditions for creating effective teams are very specific.[60]

1. There must be an identified task whose outcome can be achieved only by a collective effort.
2. This task must be clear and have measurable goals and outcomes.
3. Team membership must be exclusive; members know each other, know their roles and participate actively.

4. A team must manage and control its own processes.
5. Team membership must be stable over time.

To illustrate the importance of these conditions, imagine a symphony orchestra practicing a piece of classical music for an upcoming performance. The piece can be properly performed *only* if every musician in the orchestra practices diligently. Great individual performances will be lost if everyone doesn't attain a certain standard of performance. The task itself is clear – each note is written and must be played in a certain way – and the conductor works to ensure proper emphasis and timing. The orchestra membership is fixed; time for rehearsals is set. If everyone practices diligently, performs to the best of their ability and fulfills their commitment to the orchestra, the end result will be a rich, beautifully performed piece of classical music.

Now imagine if the conductor kept changing the piece of music and different musicians showed up at every rehearsal. What would happen if the violinists didn't bother to practice or the woodwind section kept squabbling amongst itself instead of practicing the music? What if the flutist decided that she preferred to play the French horn instead? And what if practices were held intermittently, according to the whim of the concert hall owner? The end result would be a disaster – an embarrassing cacophony of random notes!

Employees earn their place on the team by joining individual talents to the collective effort and by following through on commitments. When team members succeed in fulfilling their commitments, the experience is both productive and rewarding. Moreover, this sense of contributing to the greater good energizes people, stimulates positive relationships and facilitates improved communication. When co-workers are also friends outside of work, the relationship has a positive affect on productivity.[61]

> *If you look at one of the similarities of all winning teams, there was a family structure and closeness to the team that was pretty special...as with all families, there is usually nothing left unsaid and no hidden agendas that aren't exposed.*
>
> *- Marc Crawford, NHL Coach*[62]

Team members will put in extraordinary efforts to conquer steep learning curves and overcome seemingly insurmountable obstacles by driving themselves (and their colleagues) to greater performance. When the challenge of a nearly impossible deadline is met by a team, and that team's accomplishments receive sincere praise from organizational leaders, it demonstrates many of the behaviours necessary for "workplace trust."

The most important behaviour demonstrated, perhaps, is that of earned respect:

> Respect begets respect, and leads to trust, loyalty, openness, sharing, caring, sticking up for teammates, co-operation and other character values responsible for success.[63]

The mutual respect and trust that a successful team builds is as real and tangible to those team members as anything they have experienced at work.

If you reflect on your own "best" team experiences, you may fondly recall times when you felt completely engaged, motivated, learning, happy to come to work and pleased to be contributing to your organization's mission. What you were experiencing was workplace trust, likely accompanied by a feeling of being an integral part of your organization.

People on functional teams are given the opportunity to earn trust with their co-workers and organization. At WestJet, managers are "socialized out" of problem-solving issues, leaving it to their teams – a mixture of experienced and relatively new employees – to develop solutions. This systemic approach to empowering teams is one reason why WestJet has been able to sustain its powerful corporate culture despite growing from sixty-two employees in 1996 to 6,000 North American employees by 2007.[64]

The reason that people enjoy teamwork so much is simple. When employees are on functional teams, they are in a trust environment. They suddenly have access to information that was previously not available to them. They are encouraged to contribute their particular skills, knowledge and experience instead of simply being told what to do or how to do it. There is a free exchange of ideas that is informal, frequent and unfettered – something rarely seen in staff meetings. And it really doesn't matter what someone's title is or where they are on the organizational chart; all people want to know is "What can you contribute to the team?"

Functional teams also have a way of acting independently of the usual bureaucracy and hierarchical constraints. Perhaps because they are so focused, teams seem to find a way to circumvent the usual bureaucracy and obtain needed resources quickly. Same with access to senior management;

teams seem to open the right doors and facilitate the interactions with decision-makers in an expedited fashion.

Add to this collegial atmosphere a heightened sense of urgency and new levels of motivation and achievement become possible, even probable. When functional teams are assigned complex, high profile or urgent tasks, employees talk about experiencing a "good stress" – a combination of an exciting challenge and the motivation of a looming deadline.

The motivating effect of teamwork, applied throughout an organization, is the framework for a trust organization's culture. On an individual level, it consists of an employee's willingness to contribute skills, follow through on commitments and earn respect. On a work unit level, the five conditions for teamwork must exist and be continually reinforced. At the leadership level, an organization needs senior managers who support and encourage individual and team development above all else. In a trust organization, the "best team" you were ever on at work *is* the organization.

Beware of Imitations

Achieving the conditions necessary for functional, productive teams requires that senior managers are capable of empowering teams with certain responsibilities. In our experience, however, the ability of senior management to delegate authority, share vital information, transfer control and provide effective leadership are often limiting factors in creating an environment where teams (and trust) flourish. Instead of functional teams, therefore, employees experience the frustration of participating in "nominal" teams. Nominal teams – teams in name only – lack the vision, structure, independence, mandate and leadership necessary to enable members to contribute skills, demonstrate commitment or experience the positive aspects of being part of a functional team. Not all teams demonstrate organizational trust.

Tim's Nominal "Team"

Tim was a researcher for a large public health organization in the mid-1990s. The organization's senior management wanted to create a data warehouse, integrating the various systems that tracked patient transactions. Having all the patient data in one place would provide program managers with valuable information and allow for comparative cost analyses. An information technology (IT) firm was hired to lead the project. Its consultants met with senior managers from the public health organization to determine the project's scope and deliverables.

Following these initial meetings Tim and others from the public health organization were assigned to the Data Warehouse Project team. The team consisted of fifteen members: seven from the public health organization and eight from the IT firm. Neither Tim nor any of the other staff members assigned to the project team were present at the initial meetings between senior managers and the IT firm, nor were they briefed on the contract details.

Nonetheless, appointed staff and the IT consultants met several times over the course of a few weeks to discuss tasks and develop a work plan for the $6 million "Data Warehouse Project." The IT consultants were very keen to progress; their contract was for the first phase of the project only, and they were told that additional multi-million dollar projects were conditional upon its success. Tim and his co-workers were unaware of this condition – they were simply fulfilling professional obligations by serving on the project team.

Unfortunately, a number of things occurred during the first six months that derailed the project. First, there was no clear vision concerning the project's goal or what constituted a successful outcome. For the IT consultants, success was demonstrating sufficient progress during the first contract to attract additional contracts. For Tim and the rest of the staff, it was a vague belief that creating a data warehouse would somehow benefit the organization.

The team also contained several members who didn't have the appropriate skills to contribute meaningfully. While the IT consultants were subject-matter experts in data warehouse technology, most of the staff appointed to the project (including Tim) had little IT background and no experience with data warehousing. Not surprisingly, there was little communication or interaction between the two groups. The few staff familiar with the technical aspects of patient data resented the condescending attitudes of the IT consultants and would sometimes argue with them about very technical (and often irrelevant) data issues. These counterproductive exchanges served only to strain communication between the parties.

While the IT firm gave its consultants autonomy to control the processes – determine the project tasks, develop the timetable, commit the resources to completing the tasks, etc. – staff of the public health organization had no control over the project. Instead, Tim was called in weekly by his supervisor and grilled on his participation. "Did you attend the meetings? What tasks are you working on? When will they be completed?" The distinction between the IT firm's approach to empowering its employees and the micromanagement of staff by the public health organization managers heightened the contrasting approaches to management and served to demoralize staff.

While the consultants from the IT firm continued to press the public health staff to complete their tasks, deadlines were missed and the inevitable finger-pointing began. Tim completed the task he was assigned – a needs requirement document – but few other tasks were successfully completed. Eventually, after an expenditure of $6 million and very little progress, the project was quietly dropped. In the aftermath, senior management blamed staff for the lack of progress, quickly re-hired the IT firm for other projects and continued to award them lucrative contracts despite their non-delivery on the Data Warehouse Project.

If the public health organization had been managed by trust principles, a different outcome would have resulted. The Data Warehouse Project might have produced tangible results and been a positive, empowering experience for the staff involved if employees had been:

1. present at the initial meetings to share knowledge and develop a common vision
2. allowed to volunteer for the team
3. given responsibility for project delivery and
4. had control over the project resources.

Or, the project may not even have proceeded if, at the outset, the public health organization and the IT consulting firm had established that they could not agree on a compelling vision for creating a data warehouse. In that case, $6 million of taxpayers' money would not have been wasted and the organization's human resources might not have been squandered in such a fruitless and demoralizing project.

Unfortunately, barriers to trust exist in almost every organization. In the next chapter, we will examine the most common barriers to trust and apply trust principles to show how they can be overcome.

Chapter 8
The Bad News: Barriers to Trust Exist

Whether employed by a large company, small business or public service, most of us have experienced barriers to achieving, or fully participating in, an organizational culture based on trust principles. Although there are some rare exceptions – visionary companies like General Electric, Sony, IBM and others[65] – the vast majority of workplaces do not possess environments that maintain high levels of employee engagement, sustain productive behaviours or achieve the full potential of their workforce.

The reasons for this underperformance vary, from historical indifference to the growing number of small businesses that lack the knowledge, skills or experience necessary to develop workplace trust. Whatever the specific reason, however, the cultural and competitive landscapes are changing. Every organization, from large government ministries to fast food outlets, has to be able to hire and retain new staff, harness employees' willingness to contribute, and reward productive behaviours that sustain exceptional performance. Recognizing common barriers to workplace trust is the first positive step toward overcoming them.

Some Exceptions

The "indoctrination" of employees at IBM and Walt Disney demonstrates a visionary leader's ability to define a corporate culture, articulate values and instil certain behaviours that drive and sustain excellent performance.[66] Some companies have even institutionalized this practice, establishing "campuses" where new employees attend classes to learn an organization's history, values and expected standards of conduct. While these organizations place a high value on attracting employees who will preserve their core values, they also place a strong emphasis on giving employees opportunities to contribute their individual talents. [67]

> *"If you go to work at a visionary company, you will either fit and flourish...or you will likely be expunged like a virus...there's no middle ground.*
>
> *- Collins & Porras, Built to Last, p.9.*

Organizations with strong identities, visionary leaders and significant training resources, however, are the exception. The vast majority of us work in organizations that struggle to develop and maintain effective corporate cultures. "Average" organizations consistently experience staff engagement issues because they lack the leadership cultures, values and knowledge necessary to sustain productive behaviours over the long term. Organizations are also influenced by external factors that cause their cultures to devolve in certain directions:

1. Changing market conditions can force drastic cultural changes, as in IBM's change from selling mainframe computers to becoming a "customer-focused provider of computing solutions."
2. The industry the organization belongs to, e.g. high tech, manufacturing, fast foods, government, etc., shapes corporate structures, management practices and personnel practices.

3. A changing regulatory landscape prompts cultural change, e.g. new funding initiatives encourage competition in a previous not-for-profit sector.

> *"Top management will have an impact on an organization- in most cases, a significant impact. The question is, will it have the right kind of impact?"*
>
> *-Collins and Porras*
> *Built to Last, p.173*

It is most likely, however, that the most powerful influences determining your organization's culture are the positive and negative characteristics of its leaders and senior level managers. These attributes, and the leaders who model them, play a significant role in shaping the habits and behaviours of employees.

The Challenge of Public Sector Leadership

In our work with large public sector organizations, we find that employees' perception of a leader's ability to convey a clear vision and give clear direction strongly influences levels of engagement and perceptions of organizational trust.[68] This is something of a conundrum for senior public sector managers since obtaining clear direction from politicians is rarely a quick or simple matter. Many public policy decisions are steeped in multi-party deliberations, compromise and process. Establishing a focused, long-term vision for any public sector organization is a challenging task; communicating the vision and its practical implementation with equal clarity represents another significant challenge.

The difficulty of communicating clearly within the public sector environment is compounded by a number of inherent factors: the brief tenure in office of most senior level managers,[69] large numbers of employees, layers of bureaucracy, protocols associated with communication and multiple offices locations, to name a few.

> *For the culture of the public service to change so that regularity, propriety and good management in general are given a higher priority, the public service, and particularly those who are its administrative heads, must give management skills a higher priority.*
>
> *-excerpt from Gomery Commission*

Another challenge of corporate communication in the civil service is that the system itself does not produce many leaders with consistently strong management skills. Two noted historical weaknesses of public sector managers have been a lack of accountability and below average performance.[70] These traits have directly influenced subordinates, whose own management skills fall "short of acceptable standards."[71] Since the public service does not routinely reinforce or systematically develop managerial skills or leadership qualities, few senior managers can be expected to possess those leadership traits associated with the ability to formulate, communicate and unify employees around a powerful strategic vision.

> *"Leaders make sure people not only see the vision, they live and breathe it."*
>
> *-Jack Welch, Former CEO of General Electric*
> *Winning, p.67.*

Information Hoarding

Perhaps due to these inherent characteristics – slowly developing policy directions, communication barriers and an underemphasized leadership culture – even fewer middle managers in public sector organizations develop strong leadership skills. There is a tendency to isolate staff rather than team build. Managers rarely reward or positively reinforce top contributors and spend far too much time dealing with the "deadwood."[72] Add to this the time constraints associated with being a middle manager –- working upwards of 71 hours per week – and practicing superior communication skills becomes an untenable luxury. Few have time to formulate visions, provide on-the-job contextual knowledge or keep employees fully informed about strategic developments while struggling to perform their own jobs. It is easier to hoard information and propagate a "need to know" culture.

The Downward Spiral

The problem with a culture of information hoarding, however, is that it leads to exclusivity. When routinely excluded from meetings where knowledge sharing, problem-solving, strategy sessions and operational planning are conducted, employees lose their desire to contribute, becoming less productive and less engaged. Cutting off staff input also leads to organizational inefficiencies; managers miss valuable insights that would invariably inform strategy and streamline implementation. Chronically lacking significant staff "buy-in," some public sector organizations will experience poor resource utilization, high staff turnover, declining performance and possibly, a loss of public confidence.

Diagram 1
Effects of Information Hoarding, Exclusivity on Organizational Trust

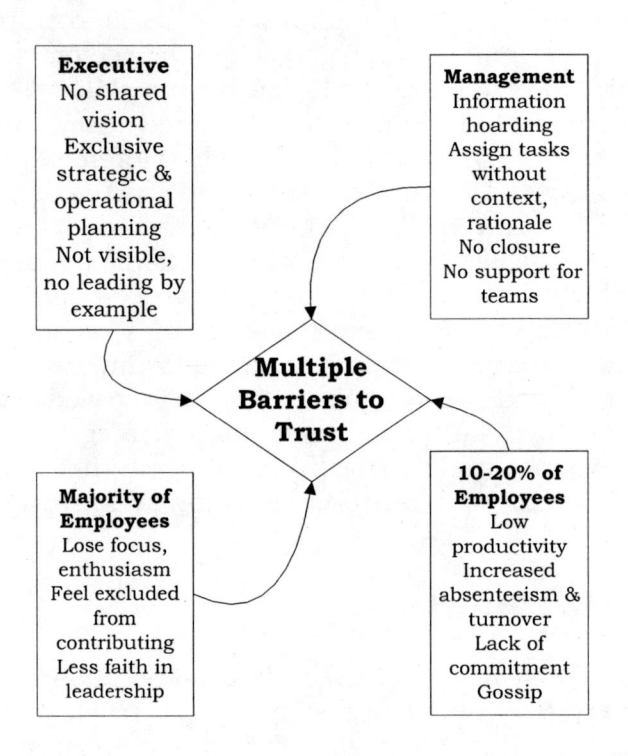

Executive
No shared vision
Exclusive strategic & operational planning
Not visible, no leading by example

Management
Information hoarding
Assign tasks without context, rationale
No closure
No support for teams

Multiple Barriers to Trust

Majority of Employees
Lose focus, enthusiasm
Feel excluded from contributing
Less faith in leadership

10-20% of Employees
Low productivity
Increased absenteeism & turnover
Lack of commitment
Gossip

The downward spiral begins at the top and works its way down to the front-line employees. Without clear communication and direction from senior levels, engaged employees have difficulty prioritizing tasks and maintaining focus. Rumours fill the gap of missing strategic information. Employees grow frustrated with the lack of contextual knowledge, particularly when managers share vital information after the fact, piecemeal or only when pressed. An employee's desire to contribute will gradually diminish with the realization that his or her input is no longer solicited or valued. The downward spiral creates multiple trust barriers, eventually crippling the organization's ability to perform.

"Out of the Loop" Liam

Liam, one of our workshop attendees, told this story about how management's unwillingness to share information alienated staff and fractured trust within an organization.

> I worked in a large public sector organization where the management team, after extensive training in the concept, adopted the "manage by objective" approach. It was a really popular management fad at the time (late 1980s). The management team met in March to determine the dozen or so objectives it would be managing toward in the upcoming fiscal year. The objectives were committed to a document and sent up to an executive committee for inclusion in the organization's overall strategic plan.
>
> The problem, from the staff's perspective, was that the discussions concerning the objectives took place in complete secrecy. Managers did not ask our input nor were the results of the discussions ever shared; no one outside the management team ever knew what our

branch's objectives were! When we asked, managers would only give us fragments of objectives. Occasionally, we were able to deduce a new emphasis based on shifting resources or through branch correspondence, but we were always behind the curve. The organization's strategic plan wasn't shared beyond the senior management level either.

The whole thing was abandoned a few months later anyway. I overheard a member of the management team complaining that the objectives changed so much during the twelve-month period, they couldn't be held accountable to them! I know the branch spent a lot of money on the "management by objective" training. In fact, few of us got any courses that year because all the managers had attended the "management by objective" training and spent most of the budget.

What I really remember about the whole exercise was how it divided the branch. The supervisors and analysts who were left out of the discussions really felt disconnected from the branch's important work. We knew after the exercise that we were not an integral part of the management team, as we had been told; the process underlined that we were just functionaries.

It was difficult to do your job properly when you really didn't know what your branch was trying to achieve or what its priorities were. It was even more difficult to stay motivated or to think of having a future with that organization when management never asked your input about a few strategic objectives.

Soon after that, I checked out mentally from my job and starting looking for opportunities elsewhere. Within a year, many of us – all of the young supervisors and analysts – had left. Those who remained were the older, close-to-retirement employees.

For Liam and his bright young colleagues, being excluded from the unit's "management by objective" exercise signalled the end of their productive time with the branch. The management team had ruptured employees' trust by:

1. excluding employees from participating in the planning exercise
2. failing to share information concerning the management objectives
3. telling support staff they were integral to the branch but demonstrating exactly the opposite
4. modeling poor management practices such as a lack of accountability, poor strategic planning skills and committing significant training resources without achieving any return on investment.

In turn, Liam and his colleagues lost their drive to contribute, becoming less engaged and marginally productive employees. Shortly after Liam left the organization, the isolationist management practices caused it to implode.

The downward spiral continued to affect the organization negatively for a decade. Over the next few months, the entire management team was disbanded – re-assigned, demoted or retired.

> *"The government has excess senior managers, and in my opinion, a deficit of senior leaders."*
>
> *-Professor Linda Duxbury*
> *Carleton University*
> *Canadian Government Executive magazine*

Incoming managers had difficulty rebuilding trust and finding qualified staff. External stakeholders who had witnessed the poor management practices, high staff turnover and lack of progress were reluctant to support the organization's directions. The branch's major initiative, supposed to be completed within five years, remains on-going after more than two decades.

Private Sector Challenges

Some of the trust barriers that plague large public sector organizations also exist in the private sector. Few small businesses [73] have clearly defined, well-communicated visions. Fewer still have leaders capable of inspiring staff or creating an engaged, productive workforce that sustains excellent performance. And very few emphasize the development of leadership skills over the day-to-day pragmatic tasks associated with creating profits. The result is almost always an underperforming organization.

Unlike the public sector, where cultural change is disassociated from market demand, increasing global competition is forcing small businesses to produce higher value-added goods and services, employ higher skilled labour, increase investment, adopt new technologies and improve productivity.[74] The stakes are high: Small business contributes twenty-three percent of Canada's GDP, represents 98.9 percent of all Canadian firms and accounts for half of the nation's jobs.[75] Failing to match competitors means fewer jobs, fewer growth opportunities and a falling standard of living.

> *"In the most common scenario, the company's mission and its values rupture due to the little crises of daily life in business."*
>
> *-Jack Welch*
> *Winning, p.21*

The ability of small businesses to evolve and to remain competitive in the longer term will depend greatly on the quality of its organizational culture. Will our culture enable us to sustain growth? Will there be sufficient trust and employee autonomy to retain top performers and attract new talent? Will everyone act like a team, creating superior services and products that engender pride while spurring innovation? Or will we be content with chaotic growth, high turnover, inconsistent people management and average performance? The ability to identify and overcome trust barriers, therefore, becomes an important cornerstone of small business strategy.

Identifying Trust Barriers

In any sector, there are many barriers, cultural and otherwise, to establishing organizational trust. To identify the barriers that exist within organizations, we have asked hundreds of employees from public sector organizations, multinational corporations and small business to list their "Top 10 Barriers to Workplace Trust©". And just as people grow animated and excited when describing their positive experiences on functional teams, so too do they become anxious and frustrated while describing their perceived barriers to trust in the workplace.[76]

We temper this difficult exercise by adding the following caveat: "For every perceived barrier to workplace trust you list, you must also suggest a way to overcome this barrier."

In every workshop, the dynamic is the same. People have no trouble listing their Top Ten Barriers to Trust©, but they always have difficulty suggesting ways to overcome these barriers. Even when this exercise is performed by highly functioning teams, the barriers always outweigh the solutions.

A typical list of barriers and strategies to overcome them is shown below:

Table 2
Top Ten Barriers to Trust & Ways to Overcome Them

TOP 10 BARRIERS TO ORGANIZATIONAL TRUST	WAYS TO OVERCOME BARRIERS
lack of a unifying theme or vision – Not knowing how the theme/vision/mission relates to my job	develop a meaningful vision that enables me to prioritize tasks
not enough information to perform my job properly	more staff meetings, training, opportunities for information sharing
lack of follow-through on commitments, poor listening skills	making people accountable, customer service training
fear of speaking up, giving honest feedback	suggestion box, surveys
lack of teamwork	Team building courses?
lack of decision-making/leadership	keep everyone informed of goals, objectives
no reward for extra effort	incentive programs, profit-sharing
negativity	avoid negative people; be positive in the workplace
gossip	don't participate
lying	make people accountable

What always emerges from this exercise is a realization that most employees are afraid to speak up and provide leaders with honest feedback. Indeed, fear is a dominant feature of most organizational cultures. Many employees are afraid to criticize the status quo, suggest alternatives or propose potential solutions. Even when asked by managers and supervisors to offer suggestions and improvements, many say past contributions have been greeted with reactions ranging from indifference to outright hostility. Some even told stories of supervisors and managers reacting with subtle threats and calculated retribution. In such environments, it is no wonder employees stop suggesting ways to improve their workplace and become disengaged from their jobs.

There are some small variations of this list, depending on an organization's particular circumstances. For example, in organizations where downsizing has recently occurred, employees fixate on specific issues related to the staff cuts – how it was communicated, who was let go, who was rehired, etc. – and report widespread distrust. Similarly, a branch that has had three different managers in one year is likely to be paralysed by a leadership void and most of its trust issues will relate to the lack of decision-making and direction. Gossip, negativity and personality conflicts dominate lists of workplaces that have been dysfunctional for a long time.

Three Common Roots

Barriers to trust can be broken down into three main categories:

> 1. barriers arising from poor communication skills

2. inconsistent leadership/management practices, and
3. a lack of personal accountability.

In the next chapter, we look at the barriers caused by poor communication skills and the strategies for overcoming these barriers.

> *"Eventually, you come to realize that people don't speak their minds because it's easier not to."*
>
> *- Jack Welch*
> *Winning, p. 29*

Chapter 9
Overcoming Communication Barriers

Communicating effectively with staff throughout an entire organization is challenging at the best of times. One reason is that we all process information differently. Some people are auditory learners; they input and comprehend information they hear much more efficiently than information they read. Others need to see the whole picture first (sometimes literally!) before understanding all the tasks associated with a project. Still other employees need to be shown "hands-on" how to do something. These tactile learners gain little from reading and trying to comprehend a policy and procedures manual.

Other reasons for communication difficulties have already been mentioned: corporate "silos," declining inter-personal communication skills, the sheer volume of e-mails and voice mails, rapidly-changing work environments and shifting job priorities. These factors blur employees' understanding of their tasks and priorities.

The most critical challenge to effective corporate communication, however, resides with an organization's management. Simply put, from top executives to supervisors, the role of every manager is to treat each employee as a valued teammate. Teammates need to know the goal toward which they are working and how their role contributes to the team's progress. They want to participate in building the team's strategy and share in the victory celebrations. When managers communicate in any manner except the inclusive, intimate dialogue of teammates, they are missing opportunities to boost staff engagement and improve productivity.

Shared Visions

In an earlier chapter, we also discussed how successful organizations like General Electric, WestJet and the Salvation Army possess "shared visions of excellence." The visions enable these high-performing organizations to define their corporate cultures, standardize productive behaviours and guide employee decision-making. What happens, however, if your organization lacks this vital starting point?

Barrier #1: Lacking a shared vision

"My organization lacks a clear, unifying vision" is consistently selected as one of the top barriers to building a productive workplace culture, based on feedback from hundreds of our workshop participants. When organizations lack this clarity of vision, employees are not always certain about their priorities, much less on how to use their talents to maximize contributions. Over time, this state of confusion drains away potentially productive energy and leads to lower employee engagement.

The "vision" issue is more fundamental than having a clear and concise slogan – it is how the vision is interpreted and implemented organizationally that determines its effectiveness. Even if people know what their organization's vision is, they sometimes get conflicting messages concerning its practical application.

"Respected Professional"

Bette is an auditor for a government department that collects provincial sales tax. Her organization recently completed a series of exercises designed to establish a "vision" for auditors in her division. Part of the rationale for this initiative was the organization's critical need to attract new staff; however, it was also part of the provincial government's broader mandate to become more "business friendly."

Months of facilitated meetings were accompanied by brainstorming sessions, team-building exercises and feedback sessions. The culmination of all these efforts resulted in the following vision: "Auditors are to be regarded by their organization as 'respected professionals' whose role is to balance fair tax recovery while providing value-added services to the business community."

Specifically, employees interpreted this phrase to mean that auditors should both continue to recover unpaid taxes from businesses and help educate those businesses on proper tax collection methods. As highly trained accountants with professional designations, the auditors seized upon this new vision as an opportunity to develop dormant consulting skills. By helping businesses become more efficient, the auditors also fulfilled the broader political mandate of adding value to the business community.

In practical terms, being a "respected professional" conveyed the notion that auditors now had opportunities to develop their judgment and discretion in deciding whether to emphasize tax recovery or consulting as a situation allowed. For example, if the first audit of a business resulted in a tax recovery of $50,000, an auditor might spend considerable time helping that business institute an improved tax collection and payment system. If a second audit recovered only $500, then the auditor had succeeded in fulfilling the public education role, using professional skills to help that business establish efficient tax collection systems.

Despite all the efforts to develop and publicize this new vision, the organizational culture did not change sufficiently to accept the auditors as they had newly defined themselves. Senior management had always looked at the bottom line of tax recovery versus money spent on audits and this metric continued to dictate behaviour. Middle managers competed internally for assignments that promised the greatest tax recovery potential, the public education role was given lip service and second audits that recovered only small amounts were considered "failures." The emphasis remained on Bette and her colleagues to recover the most tax monies in the least amount of time.

The disparity between the organization's desire to re-invent itself and its static value system produced some negative consequences. The auditors and team leaders who had spent considerable time and energy developing the "respected professional" vision grew cynical about management's ability to listen and respond to staff concerns. Many auditors, including Bette, attempted to balance the tax recovery and business advisor roles, only to receive a lack of management support for the latter. This inconsistency led to confusion and frustration on the part of some auditors, significantly lowering their engagement levels. In a job seekers' market, the organization has a difficult time competing for new staff to address current and forecasted shortages. Bette is unsure whether to stay with the organization or move on to other opportunities in a growing and competitive market.

Why did Bette's organization spend considerable time and money to develop a new "vision" and then fail to implement it? The answer lies in the product itself. To influence behaviour, a shared vision must possess certain characteristics [see Chapter 1]. The vision that Bette and her colleagues helped develop possessed most of these criteria – it came from within the organization was memorable and concise and, if interpreted as intended, enabled staff to prioritize their tasks. What was missing, however, was linking the vision and the organization's reward system to an *outcome* of excellence.

Successful organizations like WestJet link their shared vision of "we care because we're owners" to a very specific outcome:

> "By 2016, WestJet will be one of the five most successful international airlines in the world..."[77]

By linking the vision to a measurable outcome – profitability - WestJet leaders are able to reward behaviours that improve customer service and increase revenues – and discourage and eliminate behaviours that do not. By aligning corporate practices, everyone in the organization must move toward the same result.

"Process and Pay in Thirty Days"

The importance of including a measure in an organization's shared vision of excellence is not restricted to private sector organizations. An administrative section of a provincial transportation ministry responsible for processing highway construction and maintenance invoices was struggling to cope with work volume and time constraints. The invoices the department received ran several pages long and included billings for engineering services, geotechnical services, materials costs and multiple labour inputs. Each line of the invoice had to be checked for accuracy and for compliance with contractual agreements.

The seven-person unit responsible for processing these payments decided its shared vision of excellence was "all invoices will be processed and paid within thirty days." The team developed the vision as a simple way to set priorities and measure its success. It also created a consistent approach to the work – if staff are away, the remaining team members note the dates of the waiting invoices and includes them in determining their proper order. The team processes ninety-seven percent of invoices within thirty days – there is little need for supervision – and their shared vision of excellence engenders a sense of team pride.

"Protecting the Health of Our Communities"

Another public sector organization that benefited from the process of adopting a shared vision of excellence was a group of environmental health officers attached to a regional health authority in Northern British Columbia (BC).

Environmental health officers (EHO) inspect restaurant food preparation areas, approve septic systems and test municipal water systems to ensure safety for human consumption. One only has to remember the tragic events that occurred in Walkerton, Ontario to be reminded of the importance of diligent environmental health practices.[78]

With booming population growth in its region, the Northern BC EHO found itself inundated with requests to inspect a growing number of restaurants, approve septic permits for several brand new subdivisions – even give talks to community groups and schools. The volume of permits, the number of inspections and other demands for service were increasing rapidly. The group was having difficulty deciding exactly how to prioritize its work. An organizational audit confirmed that the EHO was falling behind in its workloads, barely meeting minimum regulations. Stressed and stretched beyond the limits of its resources, the team of experienced, committed professionals decided to hold an organizational retreat to address the criticisms, performance and workload issues.

The retreat began inauspiciously – the EHO was still angry over the criticisms levelled in the organizational audit. After some finger-pointing, however, people settled down to work on the issues.

After some passionate debate and much brainstorming, the EHO and its managers determined that the paramount concern was to protect the public's health in the communities the organization served. The shared vision of excellence became:

"Protecting the health of our communities."

The phrase meant that the organization gave priority to tasks that potentially protected the health of the greatest number of people. For example, a town's well water was tested before inspecting a single restaurant's food preparation area. Community waste treatment systems received priority over individual permit applications.

In this way, EHO was easily able to prioritize its workload, provide consistent service in every community, eliminate non-productive tasks (such as giving talks to schools and community groups) and have a legitimate rationale for prioritizing workloads. Six months after adopting its "shared vision of excellence," the organization reported significant efficiency gains and reduced employee stress.

The benefits stemming from the organizational retreat did not end with a shared vision. After relegating (or eliminating) many superfluous tasks, the re-energized EHO was ready to accept new challenges. With the active participation of everyone – senior managers, EHO, support staff and summer students – the organization selected a number of issues as priorities requiring completion within the following six months. Staff volunteered for tasks they felt suited their talents and experience, teams spontaneously formed, and after due consideration of their current workloads, employees publicly committed to completing assignments by a certain date. The tasks, resources and due dates were committed to a formal Action Plan document and distributed to everyone. Six months later, the tasks were all successfully completed, the organization had eliminated all the negative issues raised in the organizational audit and the Northern BC EHO was now leading the province in certain key performance measures.

The retreat provided the opportunity for the organization to complete several productive processes:

1. a candid discussion addressing criticisms, workload issues and priorities
2. developing a shared vision that enabled the prioritization of workloads

3. providing an opportunity for staff to determine operational plans and contribute toward their implementation
4. moving the entire organization forward from underachievers to leaders.

Critical to the success of this initiative, however, was the willingness of leaders to facilitate the process and the equally strong commitment of employees to carry it out.

Paige's Pages

Recently, a workshop participant named Paige offered her story concerning the importance of knowing how her job linked to her organization's vision.

> I had been working for a large supermarket chain for two years on a part-time basis. About sixty percent of the staff was part-time. I worked in many different departments – produce, grocery, bulk foods and customer service – and did a variety of tasks. If I didn't know what to do in a particular job, I would ask the assistant managers. They would always give me one or two tasks; I felt embarrassed about asking them what to do all the time. Sometimes they would even give me conflicting advice.
>
> Our store got a new manager and the first thing he did was meet with all staff individually. When it was my turn to meet the new manager, I was a bit nervous. He began the meeting by reviewing several company store policies that I already knew. Then he produced a new *Employee's Handbook* and

asked me to take it home and read it. He told me that it was very important that I read the *Employee's Handbook* before my next shift, and I committed to doing so. I'd just graduated from college, so reading a forty-page handbook didn't seem very difficult. As promised, I read over the booklet before coming to work the following day.

The *Handbook* actually provided me with a wealth of information about the organization's history, its philosophy and goals. Best of all, it contained a little phrase that explained what the sole purpose of my job was: "to sell quality groceries to our valued customers." In fact, the *Handbook* explained that it was everyone's first priority, from the manager to the clerk, "to sell quality groceries." It was as if a little light when on – from that point on, I always knew how to prioritize my work. I would help customers locate items first, ensure the shelves were stocked and retrieve items from the back room if none were on the floor. Then I'd do the secondary chores like sweeping or helping pack groceries. There are always things to do in a supermarket, and that little phrase helped me organize the order of my tasks.

A few months later, I was rushing to the storeroom to find a product for a customer when the manager asked me what I was doing. I quoted the little phrase from the *Handbook* as rationale for my actions. The manager's attitude immediately changed. Instead of questioning me further, he smiled and nodded at my explanation, said that I was absolutely correct and from that point on treated me more as a colleague than as a part-time clerk.

For the first two and a half years, I had struggled to figure out how to prioritize my tasks. Once I understood the rationale for my job, I was able to become more focused, enjoy the job more and be a better employee. Customers and co-workers began to notice my contribution more and I think I worked harder because of it.

For Paige, not knowing the ultimate purpose of her job initially prevented her from prioritizing her tasks and working independently. Like all employees, knowing the *why* enabled her to perform the *what, when* and *how* better.

Employees of organizations that lack a complete shared vision of excellence will struggle to establish priorities, manage resources consistently or achieve above average results. Senior level managers will have difficulty rewarding excellence because there is no agreement on what constitutes excellence. Once this vision has been clarified, however, the organization realizes several gains. Instead of having to micromanage employees, supervisors reward work that furthers the shared vision of excellence – and extinguish non-contributory behaviours and tasks. Employees gain the ability to prioritize tasks, work with less supervision and develop internal, competitive visions consistent with organizational values – visions that engender consistency, pride and teamwork. Everyone in the organization benefits, as do its clients and customers.

> **Trust Principle**
> Every successful organization has a shared vision of excellence (SVE).

Barrier #2: Lack of information to perform job properly

The second trust barrier related to corporate communication practices is the unwillingness of some managers to convey context and rationale to employees – the *how* and *why* of communication. It is essential, particularly when assigning complex tasks, to take the opportunity to explain the context and rationale for performing the task. Without this knowledge, employees are unable to link their efforts to furthering the organization's goals.

The Rationale for Giving Rationale

If you have ever had the opportunity to coach young children in a sport, you'll know what a rewarding experience it can be. Children are so enthusiastic that they will often begin an activity before it is fully explained. If you tell a group of six-year-old hockey players to skate around the rink three times, they will begin skating immediately – no further instruction is needed! A coach who gives the same instruction to a group of fifteen- and sixteen-year-olds, however, will often be met with withering stares, complaints and at best, reluctant compliance. The difference is that young adults need to know *why* they are doing something before deciding to commit to the task in a purposeful way. If the coach prefaces the skating drill by explaining:

1. that the team needs to improve their aerobic conditioning, and

2. improving aerobics will result in better game performances,

the individual team members will understand why the drill is necessary and commit themselves to it. Without this understanding, however, athletes will resort to performing drills half-heartedly or without the proper intensity.

> *"If you tell people where to go, but not how to get there, you'll be amazed at the results."*
>
> *-General George S. Patton*

Adults in the workplace are no different than these adolescents. Employees need to know why they are doing something, how it fits into the big picture and why it benefits them. This does not mean that a manager has to explain every little detail of a task every time. Ideally, a manager is able to provide employees with enough information to enable them to answer the "why" questions:

1. "Why am I doing this task?"
2. "Why is this important for the organization?"
3. "Why is this important to me?"

Note the differences for the employees mentioned in the examples below.

The Soda Aisle

Peter is an assistant manager at Lo-Cost, a busy local supermarket. It's an extremely hot day and he notices that the shelves on the soda aisle are nearly empty. This means lost revenue. Peter is a little perturbed; everyone knows soda sales are high on hot summer days and those soft drinks should have been on the shelves first thing this morning! Peter orders Jeff, a clerk, to bring the cases of soda from the stockroom and place them on the shelves. Peter tells Jeff to stock the shelves in the following order: Lo-Cost's private label brands first, advertised sale brands second and the national soft drink brands third. Jeff hurries to the stockroom to complete Peter's order.

Mike is an assistant manager at Valu-Foods, a busy supermarket located right down the street from Lo-Cost. It's an extremely hot day and he notices that the soda aisle shelves are nearly empty, potentially meaning lost revenue. Mike finds Alison, a clerk, and says:

"Alison, soda sales will be really high while the weather is warm and we need to get the soda from the stockroom and onto the shelves. To make the most revenue, you should stock Valu-Foods brands first, the brands on sale second and the national brands last. The more soda we sell, the higher our store revenue and the more hours I will be able to schedule you. Do you have any questions?"

Alison replies: "Yes. Do you want me to keep an eye on the soda aisle all day? If it gets low, should I stock it again?"

Mike replies: "An excellent question. Our priority – yours, mine, every supermarket employee – is to sell quality groceries to our customers. If that means keeping the soda pop aisle stocked, then that's your priority. If it means finding an item for a customer in the stockroom, then that is your priority. Whatever activity leads to selling the most groceries to our customers becomes your task. If you're ever not sure what to do next, come and ask me for help. Any other good questions like that?"

Alison: "No, that's it, thanks. I'll go get the soda now."

Both assistant managers got employees to complete the requested tasks. Peter's manner was direct, clearly communicated and resulted in quick action. Mike took more time to explain the task and to give contextual information. So why is Mike's approach better?

The answer lies in the e*ffect* that the respective assistant managers' approaches had on the two employees. Jeff gained little from the experience. He was asked to contribute only physical labour. He was not asked to think or use judgment, nor was he given any useful information to guide future decision-making. Jeff fulfills the order, unclear of why he is stocking the shelves in a particular way.

ORDER + TASK = AVERAGE EMPLOYEE

Peter keeps the information about the link between revenue and staffing levels to himself. If Jeff isn't immediately aware of the limited role he is given, he certainly senses it. After a short time, Jeff will lose his curiosity and complete his tasks competently but without enthusiasm.

Alison, by contrast, is given plenty of information, rationale and context. She knows why it is important for her to stock the shelves in a certain order (the store makes more money from the sales of its private label brand). She is reminded of the company's vision ("to sell groceries to our valued customers") and knows how her efforts will result in greater rewards for Valu-Foods and for her (greater revenue means more hours of work and a bigger pay check!) Armed with useful knowledge, context and rationale, Alison has a greater desire to contribute. She asks for the responsibility of keeping the shelves full of soda and she knows enough to perform the job properly, without being told what to do every time. Alison feels like a contributing member of the Valu-Foods staff.

TASK + RATIONALE + CONTEXT = THOUGHTFUL, CONTRIBUTING EMPLOYEE

The importance of regularly providing staff with context and rationale cannot be overstated. A manager builds trust by the simple act of sharing knowledge and by allowing employees to determine how best to use this knowledge. When an employee responds with initiative, he or she feels excitement at being able to contribute unique talents.

If this productive behaviour is reinforced and periodically rewarded, it will continue. Over time, the enthusiastic employee builds confidence and skills. If managers do not share knowledge and employees are not asked to engage their brains, however, enthusiasm, productivity and talent does not develop or progress.

Table 3 [below] illustrates the different experiences of Jeff and Alison.

Table 3
Communicating with Context and Rationale

Jeff	Alison
Able to follow orders	Able to follow orders
	Links warm weather to higher soda sales
	Understands higher profits result from selling private label brands compared to advertised brands and national soda brands
	Understands revenue from sales impacts her ability to earn income
	Understands the main priority of everyone's job
	Knows she can ask questions and that the assistant manager is approachable
	Is able to share her newfound knowledge with co-workers

The Engagement Effect

Over time, which employee is likely to be more productive and engaged?

It's not Jeff. If always treated as an unthinking labourer, Jeff will eventually become an unthinking labourer. Any enthusiasm, suggestions, extra effort or potential talent he may have possessed when he joined Lo-Cost will atrophy over time. When people feel that their contributions are not valued or welcomed, they will give up trying. Instead of bringing enthusiasm, curiosity and skill to the job, Jeff will soon be bringing the amount of effort necessary to perform the minimal requirements of his job.

Alison, by contrast, had a rewarding experience *doing exactly the same task.* Her assistant manager provided her with enough information to enable her to answer the "why" questions:

1. "Why am I doing this task?"

   My job is to sell groceries to customers. Using the knowledge gained about profit margins, I know how to stock the shelves in the correct order to maximize profits.

2. "Why is this important for the organization?"

   My activities are fulfilling the organization's mandate to "sell groceries to customers" and I am contributing directly to the store's bottom line.

3. "Why is this important to me?"

   If I sell more groceries and add value, the extra profits generated equal more scheduled hours of work and greater earnings for me. Because I know how to add value, I also feel that I am a valuable contributor to the organization.

Trust Principle
Provide staff context and rationale when assigning tasks.

Barrier #3: Lack of follow-through on commitments

The third barrier to trust linked to poor communication skills is the perception by staff that certain employees do not always follow through on their commitments. This frustrating and potentially divisive issue is not always about a lack of personal integrity or an organization's perceived "deadwood." It is about our inability to communicate with absolute certainty most of the time.

"Open Communication" is Good, Right?

The "open communication" that employees sometimes refer to – the free exchange of information, the ability to express an honest opinion or the "open door" policy of an approachable manager – are all desirable qualities. Leaving communication open-ended, however, is an undesirable quality that consistently plagues organizations.

Certainty is better

The only way to communicate effectively with everyone in your organization is to do so with certainty. To accomplish this, you must take the time to explain, listen and negotiate agreements with staff concerning each and every assignment. If this seems a bit tedious and time-wasting, consider the two examples below.

Uncertainty

At about 11 a.m., manager Steve walks over to employee Bob's cubicle and asks him to find out how many wireless headphones the department has sold last quarter. Steve tells Bob to perform this task "as quickly as possible." (Bob has retrieved this information before; he knows how to access the sales numbers from the company's database and the task shouldn't take long.)

Earlier that morning, Steve noticed Bob leaving the break room at 10:30. Bob usually takes his break at 10:00 a.m., so with a half hour coffee break, Steve figures Bob can't be too busy. Steve walks back to his office to finish off some other work, expecting Bob to stroll in with the figures at any minute.

Lunch hour comes and goes. At 3:15 p.m., Steve gets a call from Helene, the VP's secretary. She asks Steve for the latest sales figures as they need to be included in the package she is preparing to send out for tomorrow's management meeting. Steve sends Bob a terse e-mail:

"Bob, where are those sales figures? I need them right away!"

Steve is agitated and with every passing minute, grows more angry and frustrated with Bob. The nagging thoughts he was having this morning about Bob's long coffee breaks and his casual approach to work sometimes occupy Steve's mind to the point of distraction. Steve has completely lost focus on his tasks and the stress is building up into a pounding headache. Suddenly, Bob pokes his head into the office. "Hi Steve, just got your note. I will have the figures for you in a couple of minutes. I am just running a report to get the latest data."

"Bob, I need those figures immediately," Steve says testily. "They are on the agenda for tomorrow's management meeting and Helene has to circulate the agenda materials to the other managers right away. Could you please hurry and get them to me?"

"Sure." Bob strides back to his cubicle to complete the task. Five minutes later, he hands Steve a concise spreadsheet featuring a colour graph depicting the sales figures for the last quarter. He proudly hands the spreadsheet to Steve, who grabs it without even looking up.

Steve is perturbed at Bob. The quality of the work is good, but it should have been done earlier. Steve is worried that Helene has told the VP that he is responsible for the delay in circulating the agenda materials. Steve takes the spreadsheet to Helene and tries to re-focus on achieving something in the remaining hours of the day.

Bob is a little upset, too. When Steve tells him "as soon as possible," that usually means about a week's lead time. Besides, he was really busy right up until 1:00 p.m. doing a "rush" job for the VP of marketing. In fact, Bob was so busy this morning that he had only five minutes for a coffee break. He didn't like the tone of Steve's e-mail and he did a good job producing the spreadsheet and graph, like he always does. Instead of getting a big "thank you" from his boss, however, he was barely acknowledged and perfunctorily dismissed. Bob thinks maybe it's time to start looking for a new job – find a boss who appreciates his work, his attention to detail and his carefully crafted spreadsheets.

Communicating with Certainty

At 11 a.m., manager Glenda walks over to employee Bob's cubicle and asks him to find out how many wireless headphones the department has sold last quarter. She explains to Bob the information she requires is for tomorrow's management meeting and that the agenda materials are being circulated later this afternoon. Could he do his usual "excellent job" on the spreadsheets and graphs and have the information ready for her by noon today?

Bob tells Glenda that he is presently working on a "rush" job for the VP of marketing. Should he finish the current assignment or do her spreadsheet first? Then he asks if the data that Glenda wants should include just the last quarter or comparative data from previous quarters.

Glenda takes a moment to think about Bob's questions. "The VP's work is your first priority. I will talk to Helene right now and find out exactly when she needs the materials. As soon as I get a deadline, I will e-mail it to you. Secondly, I only need the data for the last quarter. We are discussing the various product lines we rolled out to see if the sales figures are close to the estimates."

Glenda returns to her office, phones Helene and asks her when, exactly, she needs the information. Helene tells her "by three this afternoon." Glenda e-mails Bob, "Bob, the spreadsheet detailing last quarter's wireless headphones sales has to be on Helene's desk by 3 p.m. today. Given your current workload, is this possible? Would you like me to find someone else to do this?"

Bob e-mails back, "Glenda, I will have the information you need by 2:00 p.m. today and will bring it to your office. See you then."

Glenda e-mails Helene, "Helene, we should have our material to you no later than 2:15 this afternoon. Please let me know if this is acceptable."

Helene responds, "Thanks Glenda, 2:15 would be great."

Glenda is satisfied with the responses from Bob and Helene and returns to the other tasks she was working on. As a busy middle manager, she doesn't have time to worry about how other people are doing their jobs. She has found it much more effective to provide staff with accurate information up front, ask them to commit to completing a given task by a certain time, and allow them the opportunity to demonstrate their abilities while earning trust. Glenda's motto is "100 percent closure leads to commitment; commitment leads to trust."

At 2:00 p.m., Bob strolls into Glenda's office and hands her a concise spreadsheet featuring a colour graph depicting the sales figures for the last quarter. He proudly hands the spreadsheet to Glenda, who reviews the work. "Bob, this is excellent, I especially like how the graph highlights the differences between estimates and actual sales. Good work. Would you like to take this to Helene yourself? After all, you should get the credit for doing all of the work."

Bob thanks her, agrees to deliver the spreadsheet to Helene and returns to his cubicle by 2:06. At 2:10, Helene sends Glenda and Bob an e-mail confirming she has received the spreadsheet. Bob is pleased with his opportunities to contribute. In fact, it has been a good day. First, the VP of marketing asked him to do an important assignment; then Glenda requested his help. And it was nice to hear that his boss appreciates his skill and attention to detail. Plus, his work is being distributed to the management team for their meeting tomorrow and will help inform their discussions. Bob feels like an integral part of the team today.

The Difference

In the first scenario, employee Bob is assigned a task with no clear due date. As soon as the real deadline is discovered, he makes an effort to complete the task quickly and accurately. Despite this, Bob leaves his manger's office feeling underappreciated. Bob also senses that Steve is unhappy with him, although he doesn't exactly know why. If this tension and unhappiness continues to build, how long will it be before Bob stops putting in the extra effort to produce quality work for Steve?

Unnecessary drama and mistrust occurred because there was no closure on Steve's communication with Bob. He tells Bob to produce the data "as soon as possible." There is no clear deadline and no discussion concerning the task itself. When the task isn't completed to Steve's satisfaction, he starts making negative, erroneous assumptions about his employee: Bob is taking half-hour coffee breaks, Bob can't be that busy, he has plenty of time to do the work but it's not important to him, etc.

This negativity affects Steve, causing him to lose focus on his work. It also affects Bob, who is not given any opportunity to explain his workload, apply his own knowledge to the sales data or feel like he is contributing his skills to the organization. Bob is simply rushing to perform another task.

In the second example, however, Glenda asks Bob to provide her with *exactly* the same information that Steve requested. She explains why she needs the information and for what purpose, enabling Bob to think about how he will perform the task. Their initial conversation – the negotiation preceding the agreement – gives Bob the chance to inform Glenda about his current workload and to ask important questions about the assignment. There is no opportunity for Glenda to make mistaken assumptions about Bob's availability or willingness to do the work.

Although they can't immediately decide when the task should be completed, Bob and Glenda make an agreement to find the information necessary to establish a firm deadline and to coordinate resources. After checking with Helene, Glenda and Bob reach a firm agreement about who is performing the task and when it is due.

They both return to their other tasks without undue stress or worry. When Bob follows through on his commitment, Glenda positively reinforces his efforts and demonstrates her appreciation of his work. No misunderstandings, no negative assumptions and no missed deadlines.

Do You Experience 100 Percent Closure?

Think about the last time you achieved 100 percent closure on workplace communication. Perhaps a recent instance where you took the time to explain a task to an employee, listened to his questions, set a mutually-agreeable deadline and praised his efforts when he followed through on his commitment. Or perhaps a manager approached you with a task, explained it by providing rationale and helpful contextual information, listened to your questions, let you consider the task in relation to your workload, accepted your commitment to perform the task at a mutually-convenient time and thanked you when you met the deadline.

If you are have difficulty thinking of an example of 100 percent closure, think of a situation where 100 percent closure was not achieved. What were the negative effects for all of the parties involved of not achieving 100 percent closure on communication?

The Pay-offs

- Taking the time to communicate with certainty – to employ 100 percent closure – virtually eliminates misunderstandings.
- Managers seeking to improve their communication skills will find 100 percent closure easy to use and a very effective communication tool.
- By enabling knowledge, intelligent questioning and active listening, employees remain interested and curious about their assignments.
- It allows employees the opportunity to develop time management skills, exercise judgment and demonstrate integrity.
- It gives employees the chance to earn trust by following through on commitments.
- It creates certainty both within an organization and externally – to clients and customers.[79]
- It separates acceptable and unacceptable behaviour, which can then be trained or actively managed.

"When it comes to acceptable behaviours, rules, and regulations, you simply cannot train enough."

-Jack Welch Winning p.151

All or Nothing

Like the name of the concept itself, an organization must either adopt the practice completely or miss out on its benefit entirely. In the latter instance, organizational leaders lose a potent weapon that virtually eliminates misunderstanding and prevents unnecessary stress.

If adopted, however, the real genius of 100 percent closure is that it fosters a culture of integrity. People will only make commitments they intend to keep; accountability works up and down the hierarchy and the entire organization sees how commitment leads naturally to trust. This practice can literally turn the fortunes of a company around.

Carlos Ghosn, former president and CEO of Nissan, talks about the corporate culture necessary to save the giant automaker:

> Build trust...those in charge have to demonstrate that they'll do what they say they'll do, and that takes time. But you have to start somewhere. Right from the beginning I made it clear that every number had to be thoroughly checked. I did not accept any report that was less than totally clear and verifiable, and I expected people to personally commit to every observation or claim they made. I set an example myself; when I announced the revival plan, I also declared that I would resign if we failed to accomplish any of the commitments we set for ourselves.[80]

> **Trust Principle**
> **All workplace communication should have certainty.**

When a significant number of employees perceive they lack a shared vision, feel excluded from contributing and experience muddled workplace communication, no amount of training, incentives, organizational renewal initiatives or other superficial changes will raise engagement scores or improve productivity. Instead, the onus of promoting a definitive vision, treating staff as valued teammates and communicating with certainty falls squarely on organizational leaders.

The paramount role of leadership is to model the trust principles and behaviours that define the entity's values and culture. The secondary role of leadership is to reward staff exemplifying these positive traits through promotions, bonuses, high profile assignments and training opportunities. The third stage is to train managers how to engage employees by continuously sharing knowledge and information, structuring inclusive activities and only communicating with certainty. The results will be exceptional performance and a sustainable corporate culture.

Trust Principle
Successful leaders model trust principles.

Chapter 10
Managing People

When employees talk about workplace barriers, discussions often revolve around relationships with their managers. "She plays favourites and I'm not one of them." "He never makes a decision." "We always know what the other is thinking; we work well together!" "When he says 'thanks, you did a good job,' I know it's sincere."

Conflict with one's supervisor/manager is one of the prime reasons people quit their job, based on a Gallup survey of one million U.S. workers. The negative effects of poor manager-employee relationships are significant: an estimated fifty percent drop in productivity and a forty-four percent loss of profitability. [81] Add in the costs of employee turnover, absenteeism, stress-related leave, etc. and an organization plagued with poor management-employee relations will struggle to be competitive or fulfill its mandate.

By contrast, employees who enjoy a friendly, trusting relationship with their manager are 2.5 times more likely to experience job satisfaction. They report being more productive and have greater engagement with customers. [82]

Who is Responsible?

Given the importance of achieving trustful, positive workplace relationships, who is ultimately responsible for developing an organization characterized by trust principles?

Opportunity to Build Trust

It should come as no surprise that owners and executives have the greatest opportunity for building workplace trust. Experienced, skilled and successful leaders understand this responsibility and rise to meet it. They proceed by helping to determine an organization's vision, core values and code of conduct. They surround themselves with a management team capable of implementing these qualities, and they relentlessly forge an organizational culture that singularly reflects and rewards the pre-determined corporate vision, values and behaviours.

> *"Trust happens when leaders are transparent, candid and keep their word. It's that simple."*
>
> *-Jack Welch*
> *Winning, p. 71*

"Visionary" leaders make no secret about their aims. They are highly visible, enthusiastic and do exactly what they say they are going to do.[83] Invariably, this type of leadership encourages the development of widespread organizational trust.

...or Bust

Unsuccessful leaders[84] play just as critical role a role in determining levels of organizational trust. A characteristic common of many dysfunctional workplaces is that their leaders know only how to rule by intimidation – bullying employees and creating a fearful environment to ensure unquestioned compliance and loyalty.

Former WorldCom CEO Bernie Ebbers and his senior executives ruled the communications giant in such a manner. While perpetrating one of the biggest accounting frauds in history, senior managers fired financial analysts and threatened internal auditors with dismissal when staff uncovered irregularities and brought them to the board's attention.[85] Employees loyal to senior management were lavishly rewarded; those who questioned decision-making were isolated, excluded and encouraged to leave the company.[86] WorldCom's autocratic leadership, characterized by exclusion and greed as it ignored market realities, crushed organizational trust. In the end, the leadership of one of "America's most hated companies"[87] was brought down by its own employees.[88]

Reflections and Rewards

A leader's style tends to be reflected throughout an organization in the practices of its managers and through its reward system. This is especially true in small businesses run by owner/managers.[89] If the workplace has a "command and control"-style leader, the rest of the organization tends to imitate and reward these behaviours. Managers and supervisors are promoted for authoritarian traits and unquestioned loyalty. If a leader prefers collaboration and coaching teams and individuals, then the corporate culture reflects and rewards this approach by promoting people with similar qualities and managerial styles.[90] Whatever values your leaders demonstrate tend to be reinforced throughout an organization by promotions, the allocation of training resources and the availability of opportunities. Leadership-driven culture strongly influences organizational practices, how people are managed and ultimately, the level of corporate performance.

Barrier #4: Favouritism

One of the characteristics of an organization that lacks visionary leadership and, consequently, an outcome-based vision, values and supporting behaviours, is that middle managers often act in their own best interests.[91] They act this way because, somewhere along their career paths, behaviours such as information hoarding, unquestioning loyalty, exclusivity, etc. – were rewarded and reinforced by promotions and opportunities. In some cases, these self-interested behaviours are known to senior executives, but ignored in the interest of bottom line results.[92] This is at best a short-term strategy, since managers who act in their own self-interest have a detrimental effect on employee engagement.

One of the most frequently cited behaviours of self-interested managers is that they engage in favouritism. Favouritism occurs when a manager promotes someone not on the basis of merit - or on any objective performance measure – but because of personal bias and usually because the promoted person is unquestioningly loyal to the manager. The manager gains a confederate to solidify his or her authority while reducing the threat of potential competitors.

Carolyn's Case

Consider the following example told to us by Carolyn, an employee of a large organization who attended one of our workshops:

Our department provides technical reviews of product prototypes. Mary, our manager, went on educational leave and selected her friend Toni to backfill the position. Normally, temporary assignments are posted and filled on a competitive basis, but for some reason this was not done in this case.

We were surprised at this selection because the manager position requires a fair breadth of technical knowledge and Toni did not have a technical background. Nonetheless, we are a seasoned team of professionals who take pride in our work. We were determined to continue to do our best for Toni and our organization.

A couple of things happened, however, that really affected staff morale. The first was when Toni, while our acting manager, competed for a senior analyst position. She failed the written test, scoring poorly on the technical skills portion of the interview. Despite a field of several technically proficient and experienced candidates (many of whom employees from our office), the senior analyst position was not filled. When Mary returned from leave, however, the firm re-ran the competition for the senior analyst position. This time Toni emerged as the successful candidate! Our organization claims that all promotions are based on merit, but this one was clearly not. And contrary to the job description, Toni was assigned strictly non-technical duties.

While people were still reeling from this event, Mary was promoted to acting general manager and Toni was selected to act as manager. This time, Toni was also given responsibility for overseeing all of the department's technical work.

When it became clear that Toni was unable to provide the level of technical feedback required, the review work was assigned to a manager from another department. This "farming out" of work caused delays and added cost to the product development process.

We also became frustrated by Toni's limited understanding of our work, particularly the senior staff who knew that their suggestions and ideas were not understood or incorporated. Eventually, the employees became so upset and angry that they felt compelled to do something about it. They approached Mary in confidence, complaining that a) Toni didn't understand their work, b) her lack of technical knowledge was causing costly and avoidable delays and c) that they were very frustrated at having to explain things to Toni three and four times, after which she *still* didn't understand the issues. Instead of acting on these complaints, Mary shared this feedback with Toni, who subtly threatened retribution against the staff who complained.

The atmosphere in the office is horrible. Senior employees are really unhappy with Mary, Toni and the entire organization for condoning this type of favouritism. How do you get ahead if your performance or technical abilities are not taken into consideration? How do you have any respect for the human resources department for enabling these practices to go on? Employees are asking themselves if senior managers don't seem to care about performance, why should we be so conscientious?

Everyone is applying for other jobs, lateral transfers – anything to get out of that office. People who used to be productive and take pride in their work are now doing the bare minimum. When it became very clear that in our department promotions are not based on what you know, but *who* you know, staff morale and productivity hit an all-time low.

David's Difference

After hearing Carolyn's tale of office favourites, David related his story:

We had the potential for a similar situation in our shop, but it was handled much differently. Our manager Carrie was going on a six-month leave, and we all wondered who would be appointed in her absence. Two weeks before she left, she called everyone in for a staff meeting. She explained that she was leaving for six months and that during her absence, each of the four senior staff members would act in her position for a month and a half. Carrie asked everyone to support the new managers in their roles and for the acting managers to continue to treat the staff with respect. Upon her return, she would be asking the staff how well they were treated! She said it jokingly but everyone got the point. She also explained that this could be viewed as a developmental opportunity for the four of us; we would all be given an equal chance to see if we liked being managers and if we were any good at it.

It actually worked out very well. Two of us really enjoyed the experience and the other two said they preferred their current positions but appreciated the opportunity to act in a managing role. Everyone agreed that it broadened their understanding of all the factors that weigh in decision-making and gave us a better appreciation of management's role. The latter two just didn't feel that they possessed the skills or aspirations to deal with the "people issues" that come with the job.

My co-worker and I really found the management experience enjoyable. We've since been offered some management training courses when spaces become available. I feel that I have some, but not all of the skills yet to be a good manager. I really enjoyed some aspects of the management position – particularly the challenge of motivating people, having to learn new skills and experiencing matters from a different perspective. I can say that the opportunity to act as a manager, even if it was only for six weeks, has been a highlight of my career so far.

David's rare and positive experience provoked a number of questions from workshop attendees:

- Did people in your office feel that the process was fair?
- Did the office run efficiently with so many short-term managers?

- Was there any resentment for senior staff who felt that they should be the acting manager exclusively?

"The entire process was so transparent that everyone thought it was fair. Perhaps because of the way it was communicated – in a staff meeting – everyone knew what to expect. It also planted the seed that we would have to be flexible over the next six months and adapt to the differing management styles. The office ran very smoothly; we had a good team to begin with and everyone worked together no matter who was acting manager. I certainly didn't see any sign of resentment. Once people got into the manager's role and saw for themselves what is was like, they could decide if it was for them or not.

What really sticks out for me, and for everyone in our office, is that we all have tremendous respect for Carrie. She demonstrated trust by giving each of us an opportunity to be the boss. There was no hidden agenda or favouritism shown; the process was completely open and fair. She even made sure everyone in the office knew what was going on and that the new managers would remain accountable to the staff. I really liked her approach. I want to be that kind of a leader."

The two contrasting examples demonstrate the key roles managers play in demonstrating trust behaviours and affecting corporate performance. In Carolyn's example, the self-serving manager may have gained an ally but the costs to the organization were high. Toni's lack of technical skill delays the product review process and raises questions about Mary's judgment, the credibility of the human resources department, the hiring process and the organization's stated value of merit-based promotions. Senior, skilled employees are no longer committed to give their best performance to the organization – productivity has decreased – and those with opportunities will be the first to leave.

In David's example, however, Carrie used her time away as a developmental opportunity for staff. Each senior employee was given an opportunity to act in a management position for an equal amount of time. The rationale for the temporary postings was known to everyone in the office and accountabilities were openly discussed. The manager's actions benefited her organization by grooming potential future managers and she strengthened her existing team by giving them more control and responsibility.

Who would you rather work for, Mary or Carrie? If the two organizations were competitors, which do you think would eventually be more successful?

Trust Principle
Successful leaders model trust principles.

Barrier #5: Lack of teamwork

As previously discussed, most employees have had the rewarding experience of being productive members of successful teams. This is possible when the conditions necessary for effective teamwork (see Chapter 6) are met. The other important factor is the role of management in empowering teams with sufficient resources and autonomy.

Generally speaking, there are two ways to empower teams. The first is to let the team manage itself. An experienced team knows who needs to be involved, what skills are required and what resources are needed. Team members will approach a leader with their strategy for implementation and request the anticipated resources. An inexperienced team requires a more active leadership approach. Such teams usually require guidance to facilitate the appropriate shared vision, help determine its composition, shape the strategy and adjust its request for resources.

In rare instances, functional teams can temporarily arise out of a leadership vacuum. Left alone or given an "unsolvable problem," a determined group of employees will voluntarily organize themselves into a team, assume roles, study a problem and risk developing an innovative solution. The absence of interference from self-serving management practices can inadvertently lead to novel approaches and new achievements. The downside to "spontaneous teams," however, is the on-going management of their product. Once successfully tested and launched, a product still has to be managed and accounted for by the same managers who had little (or nothing) do to with its achievement. Even good products and services can become compromised by mismanagement.

Welfare to Work

James offered his own experience of a team that was able to manage itself initially.

> I was hired to help a small team of civil servants develop an effective welfare-to-work program. The existing wage-subsidy program was, in our minds, a

failure. In most cases, once the wage subsidy ended, the job ended. Employees didn't receive enough training or skills in these low-level jobs to enable them to add value or land jobs elsewhere.

We decided to approach the problem not from the government's perspective of trimming the welfare rolls but from the employer's perspective of needing trained staff. Instead of paying employers to hire people temporarily, therefore, we would pay employers to train people on the job. We reasoned that, even if a person lost a job, they would still receive valuable training that would make them more employable.

Our team actively sought out representative employer associations and asked them two questions:

1. How much time and money do you need to train a person to become a productive employee in your business?
2. How much paperwork should be involved in administering such a program?

After extensive consultations with the business community, large employer associations and industry representatives, we received our answers:

1. About one year

2. $3,000 and one page.

We designed a pilot to test this idea. We hired an agent to screen welfare recipients for skills, canvassed employers for jobs and matched the two. Employers would receive their $3,000 "training credit" only if the new hires received all of their training and were employed full-time for a minimum of one year. The training plan – the skills to be taught by the employer to the new employee – was one page long and had to be signed off by both parties.

The pilot was an immediate success; every former welfare recipient was hired and trained. Their hourly wages averaged about $10, well above the existing provincial average of $6/hour. Of the few people who left their initial job, ninety-five percent were able to find their own second full-time job.

The pilot's budget was $1.7 million. After our success, we approached our executive with a request to expand the program throughout the province – with a budget of $20 million. We also asked the leaders of the business community to lobby politicians if they supported the program (they did). When the politicians heard about the program's success, we were invited by the government's executive (Cabinet) to give a presentation.

The team created a successful pilot in the absence of leadership – we were simply told to create a wage subsidy program - but we ended up with something superior. We then took the extraordinary steps of asking for more money (in an era of budgetary cutbacks) and requesting support from external lobbyists. We did this for two reasons – it prevented middle managers from killing or altering the successful formula and it allowed us a chance to establish the program along the lines of the highly successful pilot. We simply went over their heads.

Our presentation was a success and we were directed to expand the program, despite the budgetary restraints imposed on other government agencies. The first year of the full-time program was a resounding success; thousands of people were working full time while receiving valuable training, wages remained high and the government saved $44 million on welfare payments.

Eventually – and as we had feared - the program became a victim of its own success. Many claimed credit for it, altered its core values and over time it became less efficient, more costly to administer and produced a much lower benefit/cost ratio.

The reason for the program's outstanding initial success was threefold:

1. We had a small, dedicated team.

2. We tried something new and innovative, which likely prevented middle managers from interfering during the program's formative stages.
3. The pilot achieved sufficient early success to attract powerful external lobbyists.

Our team of three people produced, over the course of eighteen months, the most successful welfare-to-work program in the province's history. We were able to achieve this milestone by finding business and political leaders who empowered our team, even in the absence of leadership from our own organization.

Michelle and the Champion

Michelle listened intently to James' story before offering her own.

> I hear what James is saying – sometimes you have to look for a champion to get your projects off the ground. I chaired a cross-divisional team in a large organization. We had been talking about having a forum for employees – get people off site, have some inspirational speakers and talk about rebuilding a great organization. We'd been through some lay-offs and staff really needed some encouragement.
>
> We tried for months to get our project on the executive committee's agenda but we always seemed to get bumped at the last minute! The committee was getting very discouraged and people even stopped

showing up to meetings. Someone suggested that we find a champion for our cause – a senior manager who would listen to our proposal and possibly 'sponsor' our project by taking it to executive committee on our behalf. Another person suggested a certain individual – a senior manager named Meredith who used to meet with every staff in her division in an informal meeting that came to be known as "Muffins with Meredith". (The idea was to allow employees the chance to talk to senior managers about issues and concerns in a less formal setting.) These sessions were quite popular and Meredith seemed like a good potential sponsor.

She was, in fact, the perfect choice. She came to our next committee meeting, listened to our proposal and said she believed in what we were doing. Without being asked, she offered to take our proposal to executive. We were on the next agenda, got approved and were given an adequate budget! Meredith also volunteered to sit on the forum planning committee. She wanted to show support and be part of our project.

She got a lot of things accomplished through her direct communication style, experience and organizational connections. In addition to being a champion, she was also a good mentor to us.

If there is a lesson here, it is to search for those senior managers who share your passion. Invite them into the process and see if they will be your champion! The leadership usually exists – sometimes you just have to search for it.

> **Trust Principle**
> **Empower teams whenever possible.**

Lone Wolves

Not everyone is capable of performing in a team environment. In most organizations, there are a few employees who keep to themselves, work best individually and who purposely avoid teams or committee work. That's fine – the ability to be a reliable, contributing team player is not universal.

Most "lone wolves" are still able to make significant contributions to teams. The key is finding out what their skills and talents are, inviting them to use their strengths to support the team's work, agreeing on the extent of their contribution and recognizing their efforts. Let's say, for example, that employee Danica is brilliant with PowerPoint, having taken several courses to learn the program's various features. She has been put on teams before and has never felt comfortable with the dynamics. Danica prefers to work alone. Asking her to sit through team meetings, participate in brainstorming sessions and socialize with the other team members is non-productive and difficult for her. (It also frustrates team members who sense her reluctance to join in.) Instead, the team leader approaches Danica, explains the project and asks her to consider editing the team's final PowerPoint presentation by a specific date. Danica considers the request and because she enjoys working on PowerPoint presentations and is confident in her abilities, agrees to produce the final presentation by the given date. The final product is a reflection of various strengths. The team provides the expert content and Danica presents it in a compelling, multi-media format that informs the organization's decision-making.

Most successful teams are small and have a broad range of personality types, skills, talents and experience. The most fundamental rule to achieving team success is having members perform tasks that optimize their talents.

While "lone wolves" may be willing to offer their skills to help a team independently, other types of employees are not welcomed by teams. The list of people who do not add value to teams include those unable to follow through on commitments, overly critical and negative people, staff who are inflexible and those who put their own interests above the team's. Teams tend to be very selective about their membership. Over time, people not helping the team are either asked to leave or opt out themselves. This is a natural and healthy dynamic.

Trust Barrier #6: Lack of decision-making

There is a current management theory that states "...never make a decision today that can reasonably be put off to tomorrow."[93]

> *"On a really good team the role players- the foot soldiers- stand out to me. You can't have enough of them.*
>
> *-Scotty Bowman*
> *Successful NHL Coach*
> *Simply the Best, p.261*

While this theory may work effectively in certain circumstances, few things are more frustrating for outcome-driven employees than a manger or supervisor who is unable or unwilling to make a decision.

Indeed, one of the most significant factors in determining job satisfaction and organizational commitment is the perception of decision-making. In a 2006 survey of 14,000+ civil servants, some of the lowest scores were given in response to the statement, "Executives in my organization make effective and timely decisions." The survey correctly notes this low score "...represents the greatest opportunity for making positive changes."[94]

Indecision is Costly

One of the greatest historical examples of costly indecision was the policy of appeasement[95] that the British, French and Soviet governments followed during the 1930s. The great powers delayed making a number of key decisions – rearming, confronting Hitler, preparing for conflict – that eventually threatened their very existence and cost millions of lives. Although the policy of appeasement was not based merely on indecision, the lack of bold political decision-making contributed to the costly war ahead.

Great Expectations

Employees expect their bosses to make decisions. They are constantly looking to them for information, guidance leadership and...a decision. "It's the reason bosses get paid the big bucks" is a common employee sentiment.

Management experts offer the same advice: "Leaders have the courage to make unpopular decisions and gut calls."[96] IBM Leadership competencies include "Team Leadership" and "Decisiveness."[97] Peter Drucker adds:

> Decisions are made at every level of the organization beginning with individual professional contributors and front-line supervisors... Making good decisions is a crucial skill at every level. It needs to be taught explicitly to everyone in organizations that are based on knowledge.[98]

There is no great mystery involving good decision-making. Drucker talks about taking responsibility for decisions, communicating them with certainty and reviewing them periodically. One of the errors that indecisive managers often make, however, is failing to admit when they lack the information necessary to make a decision.

"I Don't Know..."

The phrase "I don't know" (if true) is a perfectly acceptable answer for a manager to relay to employees concerning a non-decision. Managers are often afraid to admit to employees that they lack such information for fear of appearing incompetent. However, revealing an honest state of affairs – being candid – helps build workplace trust. An even better answer is "I don't know...but I will let you know as soon as I find out." This allows employees to prioritize their work and continue with other tasks while awaiting direction in one area. Again, it is about communicating context and rationale and always pursuing certainty that engages employees and leads to extra effort.

> **Trust Principle**
> **All workplace communication should have certainty.**

Trust Barrier #7: Lack of rewards

Rightly or wrongly, some employees perceive that their efforts at work are generally unappreciated and unrewarded. Yes, they receive a salary, a paid vacation, perhaps even benefits, but they still believe themselves to be undervalued.

Effective leaders do not attempt to understand or judge such behaviour. Instead, they attempt to manipulate it by positively reinforcing certain actions and ignoring or negatively reinforcing others.

The Power of Positive Reinforcement

Positively reinforcing certain behaviours is a powerful strategy that can affect entire organizations. In the mid-1970s, a major courier company was having huge problems with absenteeism and people being late for their shifts. In the overnight delivery business, there is a significant loss of revenue when employees habitually miss shifts or show up late. Customers complained about the level of service they were receiving and were unhappy with the company. The situation had grown so bad, in fact, that the company was close to bankruptcy.

To reverse its fortunes, the company applied a unique solution. If employees showed up to work on time, they received a playing card from a deck. If they punctually attended all of their shifts in a week, they had five cards, enough to make a poker hand. (If they were late once or missed a shift, however, they were ineligible to play.) At the end of the week, the employee with the best poker hand won a pot of $50.

By reinforcing attendance and punctuality – for a mere chance to win a prize – the company virtually eliminated its absenteeism and tardiness problem. The company was able to reduce losses, regain customer loyalty, grow and innovate. Today, it is among the most successful organizations in the multi-billion-dollar delivery business.

Other organizations reward positive behaviours by distributing bonuses, awarding trips, offering paid sabbaticals, paid educational leaves and other incentives. Examples of punishment – trying to make unwanted behaviours disappear - include verbal and written warnings, suspensions, investigating alleged misconduct or termination. It is possible, in any organization, to align rewards with desired behaviours and punishments with undesirable ones.

It is also possible to influence behaviours through non-monetary means. The simple act of acknowledging and sincerely thanking an employee for an extraordinary effort will often serve to continue such efforts. Conversely, locking the conference room door at the precise time a meeting is scheduled to start will discourage people from habitually showing up late.

Trust organizations determine the behaviours they wish to encourage in advance, align their reward systems accordingly, and consistently reinforce or extinguish behaviours in accordance with their core values. Average organizations routinely fail at this – by not defining core values clearly, by manipulating reward systems and by inconsistently applying positive and negative reinforcement.[99]

In the Absence of Visionary Leadership – Opportunity

Familiar barriers to workplace trust – favouritism, a lack of teamwork and a lack of decision-making – appear in organizations lacking a strong leadership culture. Within such organizations, however, are opportunities for managers to demonstrate strong leadership skills that dispel any notion of favouritism, ways for teams to seek empowerment by crafting innovative products and services that appeal directly to leaders, and strategies for supervisors to improve decision-making by admitting limitations while continuing to communicate with certainty.

...and Frustration!

It is also possible, in these very same organizations, to encounter leaders who rule by intimidation, surround themselves with unscrupulous confederates, lack the ability to empower teams, and frustrate staff with indecision. While leaders bear the most responsibility for developing a trust culture and modeling trust behaviours, the ultimate accountability, as you will read in the next chapter, rests with you.

Chapter 11
Barriers to Trust: Lack of Personal Accountability

The last three barriers to workplace trust that employees frequently mention are negativity, gossip and lying (with intent to deceive). When an organization has been dysfunctional for a long time, these particular behaviours seem to be prevalent and contribute to an unproductive, unhealthy work environment.

Unlike some of the other barriers – no unifying vision, lacking information essential to job performance or communication uncertainty – these particular barriers tend to be more subjective. So often we react without knowing all the information or with a pre-determined bias. One has to remember, too, that the barriers to trust that some employees perceive are just that – *perceptions* of barriers. Sometimes individuals need to check if their understanding of an event is reasonable, complete and factual. For example, if the boss habitually goes for coffee with the same circle of friends, this is not favouritism; she simply identifies with this social group. It becomes problematic only if she excludes other employees when distributing relevant workplace information or if these same friends undeservedly receive the majority of training opportunities, bonuses or promotions. While it is always best to trust your gut instincts, it is also helpful to step back from a situation temporarily and ensure that you possess all the pertinent facts before forming an opinion or deciding upon a particular course of action.

The other thread common to these particular barriers is that they all involve a high degree of personal accountability. Only you can choose to gossip about a co-worker, deliberately lie to your boss or maintain a negative, cynical attitude. And only you can choose whether to change unproductive habits and attitudes or not.

Eliminating these particular barriers is not easy. It involves self-awareness, changing old habits and developing a strong commitment to new values. It helps, however, if everyone in the organization is on the same page.

Modeling Personal Accountability

How does an organization model personal accountability? How do leaders get employees to adopt productive attitudes and behaviours?

When planes land in Calgary, Alberta – WestJet's corporate headquarters – it is not unusual to see members of the senior management team walking through aircraft and cleaning up after the passengers disembark. This simple act, repeated almost daily, sends a profound message to staff. First, there is no task too mundane or beneath anyone's position; instead, there is a shared responsibility to ensure passenger comfort and safety that all employees should take seriously. Secondly, as they lead by example, senior managers are embodying the organization's core values of prideful ownership and dedication. They are reflecting the "hard work and devotion of all WestJetters on a daily basis..." Thirdly, and perhaps most importantly, the organization's leadership is demonstrating personal accountability. They are not just talking about appreciating WestJet guests or providing a friendly, caring atmosphere; they are actually making it happen.

The Average Way...

Contrasting the unifying leadership of WestJet is Air Canada – Canada's other national airline. Ever since the airline managed to regain profitability after near bankruptcy forced it to re-finance and restructure in 2004[100], it has shown it needs to go a long way to rebuild positive relationships with its employees. A recent survey of 900 Air Canada pilots showed that pilots perceive company leadership to be unfair and untrustworthy, and that the work environment is very negative.[101] They identify themselves as professional pilots rather than Air Canada employees – they are neither loyal nor committed to the company – and they remain with Air Canada mainly because of the limited employment opportunities for commercial pilots in Canada.[102]

How did Air Canada's pilots – for the most part senior, well-compensated staff – get to be so negative, disloyal and untrusting of their employer? While the survey did not directly address this issue, a few areas of contention emerge. Pilots believe that the $6 billion in salary concessions they offered up while the company was losing money needs to be paid back. The pilots also dislike the way their work is scheduled, believing the process to be disrespectful. Finally, pilots feel management is unsupportive and, consequently, they have withdrawn their trust from management.

What do the pilots gain from their negative attitude? What does the company gain by having a significant number of negative, unengaged employees with unresolved issues?

The answer, of course, is "nothing" – neither side gains anything and in the competitive airline industry, lower productivity can spell the difference between flying and being permanently grounded.

Workplace Negativity

Workplace negativity arises from a number of factors – increased stress and demand for services amid fewer resources, the perception of being unappreciated by the employer and the perceived inability to affect change to the "system." The widespread negativity prevalent in some organizations is not confined to rank and file labourers or minimum wage employees. Highly skilled professionals experience it – for example, emergency room physicians unhappy about staff levels, workplace stress, wage cutbacks or their ability to provide adequate patient care.[103]

Addressing these issues organizationally requires a comprehensive, long-term approach (see Chapter 12) that involves transforming an average organization into a trust organization through a series of steps – developing a leadership culture by the extensive use of leading by example, facilitating a shared vision of excellence, engaging staff through operational planning, etc. The topic of concern here, however, is dealing with negative individuals in the workplace.

Barrier #8: Negative employees

We have all had the uncomfortable experience of working with negative people – those oppositional employees who resist suggestions and even assignments. For some unfortunate people, being negative and pessimistic is a dominant part of their personality. For others, however, negative attitudes develop over time. These employees often characterize themselves as victims. Their unhappy situation is due to the "system," the boss, society, demographics – any external factor except their own actions, attitude and choices. However prolonged negativity manifests itself, the popular solution is to avoid such people at all costs. It's okay to be empathetic for a little while, but you shouldn't really waste your time or energy on them.

The Negativity Virus

Negativity in a workplace spreads like a virus; it begins with one individual and if unchecked, spreads rapidly to infect others. A trust organization takes a preventive approach to ward off 'staff infection.' Rather than ignoring or marginalizing chronically negative employees, they should be "progressively disciplined," terminated or otherwise encouraged to move on – immediately. The phrase "progressive discipline" refers to procedures – usually outlined in collective bargaining agreements, employment contracts or labour relations legislation – intended to warn, change the behaviour of, or as a last resort, fire incompetent or underperforming employees. In unionized environments, however, these procedures are usually so onerous that individual managers haven't the time, skill or patience to implement them. Instead, the negative employees are moved from job to job or given reduced responsibilities. They continue to cause drama, waste management resources and set poor examples for performance.

In non-unionized environments, negative people tend to be more effectively managed. One pro-active means of dealing with underperformers is used by the highly successful entrepreneur Jimmy Pattison. In his car dealerships, Pattison terminates new salesmen after a few months if they continue to sell the fewest cars. The notoriety of this practice misses its underlying humanity – why would you want to work for an organization where you are its worst performer? Why would you begin a career in sales if you are probably destined to be a failure at it? Why allow negativity to take root and flourish? Isn't it much better, over the long term, to find a job or build a career where you can be a success?

The 3 a.m. Acid Test

In the absence of such performance metrics, employees have to assume personal responsibility for their attitudes and performance. Give yourself this simple self-assessment quiz:

1. Do you identity with and admire some of the organization's staff, management and leaders?
2. Do you share the organization's values and still take pride in furthering its mission?
3. Can you succeed, according to your own definition of success, in your present organization?

If you honestly answer "no" to these questions and circumstances are unlikely to change soon, it's time to move on. Even the most enthusiastic, optimistic employees become discouraged if they feel their contribution is no longer valued. And if you find yourself lying awake at 3 a.m. every morning because you dread the prospect of going into work, you owe it to yourself (and others) to explore all opportunities. Otherwise, your unhappiness and stress will soon infect your personal and professional life, turning you into that unwanted negative employee or worse, a self-pitying "victim."

Negativity vs. Scepticism

While negativity is an unhealthy state that is to be avoided, employees who maintain a healthy measure of scepticism can often make productive contributions. Hierarchical organizations can sometimes be prone to a dynamic known as "groupthink." The term, coined by social psychologist Irving Janis in 1972, refers to a group making faulty decisions because they are insulated from diverse opinions. Members shield leaders from opposing viewpoints and group members are afraid to voice objections.[1] The classic example cited for this phenomenon is the Bay of Pigs fiasco, where sensible opposition to the U.S. government's ill-planned attack on Cuba was eliminated due to "groupthink" dynamics. Trust organizations, and particularly teams, embrace scepticism when it leads to the productive re-evaluation of assumptions, enhanced clarity and improved outcomes.

Barrier #9: Gossip in the workplace

Gossip is known in every society throughout the world. In North America, we are inundated with it in our media – tabloid newspapers, gossip columnists, "entertainment" TV. We know that it's bad to gossip about someone, yet most of us engage in it.

What, exactly, is gossip?

Gossip is a form of social control. Societies use it to control or modify the behaviour of others. People gossip about their neighbours to turn others against them, to pressure them into conformity or perhaps to enforce their version of acceptable social mores. Media will often try to paint an individual in an unflattering light to turn popular opinion against him. The recent coverage of the Conrad Black prosecution is a case in point. We all listen to gossip or actively partake in it. The problem is that gossip does not belong in our offices.

The Gossip

Imagine that colleagues Catherine and Richard are competing for a promotion. One day in the coffee room, Catherine casually mentions to her co-workers that she believes Richard and his administrative assistant Sally are having an extramarital affair. Catherine expresses contempt for this type of behaviour and wonders aloud if Richard's wife and Sally's husband would approve if their 'affair' were discovered. She also cautions her co-workers that "you didn't hear this from me" and that "we shouldn't say anything to anyone about this."

Of course, this is such a hot piece of gossip that Catherine's co-workers immediately set about telling everyone in the office about Richard and Sally's 'alleged' affair. At this point, it doesn't really matter that Catherine fabricated the story. The rumour has taken on a life of its own and people are usually willing to assume the worst. Now everyone in the office is suddenly keeping a watchful eye on Richard and Sally. The two are starting to feel uncomfortable as they become increasingly aware that all their movements and conversations are being scrutinized by nearly everyone in the office, and that people appear to be talking about them.

Richard e-mails Sally: "What is going on? Why are people staring at us?"

Sally replies: "I don't know. I think we should stop having coffee together every morning."

Richard: "But I need those coffee meetings to get organised! We always set out our priorities for the day. Who is going to keep me on track?"

Sally: "Sorry, but people are acting strangely. I think we should only meet at the office. I know we always get interrupted here, but I just don't need any trouble right now."

Catherine, aided by her gossip-hungry co-workers, has succeeded. She has controlled Richard and Sally's behaviour, first by causing them to be uncomfortable and stressed and secondly by limiting their meetings, thus disrupting Richard's ability to get organized.

In this scenario, Catherine and every person who participated in the gossip, either by spreading it or by acting upon it is guilty of a cowardly, malicious act. While the rumours may have only a marginal impact on Richard's (and possibly Sally's) productivity, the fact remains that all gossip is damaging and almost none of it is accurate. Insecure, envious people employ gossip as a form of social control and use it as a weapon. If unchecked, gossip will destroy trust, divide co-workers and perpetuate a toxic work environment. Gossip should never be tolerated in the workplace.

A Variation

A similar type of behaviour is sometimes referred to as "triangulation." In triangulation, Employee A has a conflict with Employee B. Instead of talking directly to B to resolve the matter, however, A goes to a third employee, Employee C. Employees A and C then confront Employee B about the issue. B feels outnumbered, threatened and defensive. "Why didn't A talk to me about this in the first place? We could have resolved this without involving anyone else. Who else in the office is taking A's side?" The similarity to gossip is that people are hearing only one side of the story and acting upon it to a co-worker's detriment.

"Not Interested"

There are three steps involved in changing gossiping behaviour:

1. awareness of the negative behaviour
2. extinguishing the inappropriate behaviour through feedback and
3. providing a positive alternative.

One way to limit gossip or triangulation is simply not to participate. No matter how tempted you are to listen or to become involved, you politely (yet firmly) state that you are not interested in hearing any gossip or rumours. This requires self-discipline and empathy. The discipline is curbing our natural desire to want to hear embarrassing stories about someone else or to want to gang up on an unpopular co-worker. The empathy is about putting yourself in that person's place. Do you want people spreading embarrassing stories about you behind your back? Wouldn't you prefer if people had the decency to talk directly with you to find out the truth or to resolve any issues they might have with you? Of course you would – you deserve to be treated with respect – and so does the person that everyone is talking about or ganging up on.

The second way to limit gossip is to direct people to the source. "Hey, why don't you ask Richard if that's true?" Gossip requires an audience and not providing an audience is an effective way to limit its spread.

Some teams use yet another method to minimize or eliminate gossip, adopting a "no gossip rule" in a team charter or code of conduct document. This is usually very effective because in a small group it's easier to identify and limit sources of gossip as they arise. Individuals are made responsible for their own behaviour, and the dynamics of working in a small team reinforce gossip avoidance. People need continuous feedback to curb their desires to gossip and supportive team members often provide the appropriate responses to extinguish or at least limit the destructive rumour mongering. Once teammates sensitize each other to gossip and have success eliminating it from their activities, it becomes easier to adopt this practice within a larger group and eventually, throughout the organization.

Not reinforcing poor behaviour is one way to identify and reduce it. Seeking a positive alternative is the logical next step. If a co-worker begins venting to you about the boss, it's okay to say, "Look, if you have an issue with the boss, talk to the boss about it." Another strategy, however, is to try to help your co-worker solve the problem. "I hear what you are saying and had a similar issue with the boss three months ago. I resolved the issue by including a business case along with the proposal and got the necessary approvals in two weeks." Teamwork: 1 Gossip: 0.

Barrier #10: Lying

Just like gossip, lying is a common societal practice. Some studies estimate that we lie about twenty-five percent of the time, mostly to make things easier for ourselves by avoiding conflict or sparing someone else's feelings.[104] This latter reason for lying – the telling of "white" lies – is not of great concern. As part of the human condition, it does not seem to be particularly hurtful or unduly disruptive in the workplace. Lying to deliberately deceive a co-worker for one's own advantage, however, is a destructive behaviour that has long-term implications for organizational trust.

Most human beings are trustworthy. In an unpublished study recently performed at a Canadian university, a participant left a $20 bill at a bus stop then wandered a short distance away. A few minutes later, he returned to the bus stop, asking the person standing at the bus stop (the subject) if he of she had seen a $20 bill. Eighty-seven percent of the subjects – all strangers to the participant – admitted seeing the $20 bill and returned it to the participant immediately.

At the workplace, most of us naturally extend our trust to co-workers, supervisors and leaders. We place ourselves in positions of vulnerability because we expect cooperative behaviour and reciprocated loyalty. What happens, however, when people lie and this trust is deliberately betrayed?

Betrayal

Betrayal is the antithesis of workplace trust.

It is a fact of human nature that people will remember, in vivid detail and years after the actual event, the time when a supervisor took credit for their work, when they were passed over for a promotion in favour of a much less qualified candidate, when they were promised a reward that never materialized or when they were otherwise betrayed by someone in authority at their workplace.

If you ask a group of employees drawn from average organizations if they have ever experienced workplace betrayal, most will answer "yes" and have a story to tell. Len's anecdote was most revealing:

> I was away the day we held our "wrap-up" meeting with the client. We had worked on their project, a restaurant redesign and renovation, for over a year. I was the project manager and had poured all my energy into the project. I really understood the client's needs and we really nailed it. The client was very happy with the results and the client's business had increased significantly. Our company president even attended the meeting; I guess everyone likes to be part of a successful project.
>
> A week after the meeting, my assistant, Ian, got promoted over me. I was very upset and phoned our division VP. He said that the president was really impressed with Ian's work on the project and that's why he was given the promotion. I told him that I had provided all the concepts executed the project plan and had done most of the work – that Ian had only taken orders. The VP said that at the wrap-up meeting, Ian had taken credit for almost the entire project and that his promotion was already a "done deal."
>
> Two years later, the exact same situation arose, except it was reversed. I had been loaned to a team to help them complete a project – I basically helped the team leader

finish the last few tasks. When she was unable to attend the final project meeting, I showed up and, seeing that the clients were pretty happy, exaggerated my contribution to the project. Sure enough, I was promoted shortly afterwards. I felt badly about it for a while, but so what? Who says life is fair?

Sarah's story involved the false promise of her manager.

> A manager writing our department's policy and procedures manual left the organization abruptly. My manager was under pressure to have the manual completed, so he approached me about taking on the task in addition to my regular workload. I agreed to perform the extra work if he would ask human resources (HR) to consider reclassifying my position. After all, I was going to be doing a manager's work; wasn't an incremental increase appropriate? He agreed that it was and I immediately proceeded to work on the manual.
>
> About two months later, I happened to be over at HR on a separate matter and, remembering my pending reclassification request, asked the HR director how it was proceeding. She looked rather puzzled; she said they were working on a number of reclassifications but none had been submitted for my position. I was really angry about this, because I had done a lot of work on the manual and was putting in a lot of extra time.
>
> When I got back to the office, I wasn't sure if there had been a mistake or not – maybe my boss had simply forgotten to forward the appropriate paperwork to HR? To give him the

benefit of the doubt, I wrote him a memo reminding him of our agreement and explaining that I was stopping work on the policy and procedures manual until the reclassification issue had been rectified. It wasn't just about the classification issue. There were nine other detailed reasons why the manual was being delayed, and most of them had to do with a lack of management commitment to the project.

For days, weeks even, nothing happened...then, I got called into the executive director's office. My boss was there and he told me to sit down. Then he started to grill me in front of his boss: Where is the policy and procedures manual? Why wasn't it finished? When could he expect it? He was very agitated and I could tell that he was under pressure to have the manual completed.

I calmly asked him if he had read my memo dated about three weeks ago. He said he hadn't, so I excused myself to retrieve a copy. Moments later, I came back with the memo and handed copies to my boss and the executive director. After reading through the memo, the executive director asked me to leave. Then he proceeded to yell at my boss.

When my boss got back to his office, he sent me a very angrily worded e-mail to the effect that I was playing a dangerous game and that if I ever embarrassed him like that again, he would make my life miserable.

I was already miserable. I'd told my husband about my potential promotion and now it wasn't true. Worse, my boss had lied to me, tried to embarrass me in front of the executive director and tried to blame and threaten me when his own actions got him in trouble. How could things get any worse?

Two months later I found a job outside that organization – a promotion, actually – and never looked back.

It was a shocking experience for me, being lied to by someone I trusted, and it stuck with me for a long time. If there was one positive, it was the lesson to never, ever treat employees like that boss treated me. When I became a manager, I made it a point to be very open with staff, to explain the reasons for decisions and to treat people more like teammates than direct reports.

Later, I heard that my old manager was demoted and eventually given a position without staff. That organization still has major trust issues. People don't forget that easily.

As these two anecdotes suggest, intentionally deceiving people may bring temporary gains. The long-term effects, however, are negative and persistent. Either a stressful, perversely competitive corporate culture emerges or employees remember instances of betrayal for years, learning to withhold trust and thereby limiting loyalty, engagement and productivity. Betraying another employee's trust is a damaging practice successful organizations seek to eliminate.

Know the Facts

As mentioned earlier, however, the *perception* of deceit rather than the actual occurrence of deception can also lead to misunderstandings and mistrust.

At a recent forum on Cultural Change held by a large public sector organization, a woman stood up and related the following story.

> A few months ago, our building had a bomb scare. Of course, we didn't find out about it from our executive. I was out on my break at a coffee shop down the street. The cashier was watching TV and as I walked in she said, "Wow – a bomb threat in your building. That's really scary!" I was shocked – I knew nothing about a bomb threat. I had only gotten an email talking about some low level threat and asking people to leave the building in an orderly manner and return in a couple of hours. I didn't even know we were in danger.

The facilitator asked if anyone from the executive would be able to answer this employee's concerns. After an uncomfortable silence, one of the senior managers stood up:

> Yes, I would like to tell everybody in the room about this incident and to clear up any possible misunderstandings. We received a bomb threat on that morning. As per our protocol, we immediately contacted the police who advised us not to panic as they considered it a very low level threat. Our procedure for this situation is:
>
> 1. inform all employees about any potential threat
> 2. evacuate the building, keeping in mind the potential severity of the threat and avoiding any panic that may cause

employees to rush for the exits and possibly injure themselves or others
3. search the building for any suspicious packages, and
4. when the search is completed and the building is secured, allow employees to return.

We did not want to stress anyone, or cause injuries by panicking people. So, we sent employees the email, informing them of the low level threat and asking them to leave the building in an orderly manner. We then had every room in the building checked for any suspicious packages - found nothing - and decided to allow employees to return to their desks and offices. Unfortunately, the media got hold of the bomb threat story and leaked it without knowing all the facts.

We want all of you to know that employee safety is our biggest concern. We followed the procedures exactly as the safety committee set them out, executed them quickly and felt confident in our decisions. We believed the threat was virtually non-existent and that the bigger threat was the potential of people panicking and trampling each other trying to exit the building. I am grateful to that employee for standing up and relating her concerns.

The moment the employees heard the calm, rational explanation – and the leadership's obvious concern for employee safety - the mood in the room changed dramatically. Employees who were angry and prepared to see the 'bomb scare' as another reason to withhold trust from organizational leaders suddenly understood the reasoning behind the actions. Armed with the facts, employees realized that the potentially traumatic event was handled perfectly by their leadership. After the senior executive sat down, spontaneous applause broke out. The facilitator pointed out that giving employees adequate background information about an action or decision – providing them context and rationale – always serves to eliminate false assumptions and to build workplace trust.

The barriers of negativity, gossip and lying to deceive co-workers all involve aspects of personal accountability and choice. We choose to react negatively or allow a situation to shut off our optimism and positive energy. We either participate in malicious, inaccurate gossip about co-workers or retain our respect and distance ourselves from it. We can lie to employees and temporarily gain an opportunity, or we can treat employees with dignity, provide them with knowledge and information, and earn their trust and respect for years.

> **Trust Principle**
> **Successful organizations abide by a code of conduct that is created by employees, known by all and modeled by leaders.**

The next chapter, the final one, will show you how to put trust principles to work in your organization whether it is large or small, private or public sector, average or extraordinary.

Chapter 12
Getting Started

Over the past eleven chapters, we have looked at a variety of issues concerning the critical importance of establishing and maintaining a trustful workplace. We believe it is a matter of trust or bust.

We've outlined seven principles required to create and sustain a trust organization.

We've acknowledged that organizational cultures do not change overnight. They change only when certain rules are adopted and a standard of behaviour is consistently reinforced.

The current problems in the workplace – low employee engagement, increased stress, declining relative productivity – are not going away. In fact, coming demographic changes will exacerbate current problems and raise the cost of retaining and attracting talent.

We've noted the differences between competitive, sustainable trust organizations and average organizations in the key areas of leadership, management and communication skills.

We've described the experience of three individuals seeking organizational trust. The first finds it and enjoys a mutually-beneficial working relationship with his boss, the second seeks vainly for trust and the third experiences a betrayal of trust. These stories illustrate how the presence or absence of trust profoundly affects an individual's productivity and engagement.

The vast majority of employees enjoy working on functional teams. If an organization is capable of supporting teams, it is capable of having a trust-based culture.

Inconsistent management practices cause multiple barriers to trust. At the same time, everyone has a responsibility to be accountable and professional – or to leave the organization.

Now it's time to get everyone in the organization involved and committed to creating a happier, sustainable, inclusive and more productive workplace.

Setting the Stage

Before you begin the process of building workplace trust, it is important to know what is happening in an organization. If an organization has recently experienced a crisis – an incidence of workplace violence, significant downsizing or public criticism – employees are likely to be angry, anxious and preoccupied with it. They will be focused more on coping with their immediate situation than on trying to learn new skills or create more effective relationships. Similarly, employees of an organization with long-standing, unresolved issues will be more interested in rehashing old grievances than in committing to new behaviours centred on standards of professionalism or personal accountabilities.

In both these situations, it is important to acknowledge the event or issues first – talk about the elephant in the room – and listen carefully to management's and employees' concerns. It is equally important not to attempt to provide a rationale for the event or to attempt to solve the contentious issues raised; that work comes later.

Step 1: Assessing engagement

Assuming that an organization is not in crisis but is wishing to improve its productivity by investing in training,[105] the first stage is to assess employee engagement. Employee engagement can be quantified through a formal survey – the Gallup survey instrument known as Q12 is an excellent example – and supplemented by interviewing staff from various levels. Leaders are often able to provide a strategic overview of the organization's recent past and future; most managers have a reasonably good grasp of their employees' performance; front-line workers offer up their perspective concerning the issues directly affecting their engagement, loyalty and commitment.

The "20-70-10" rule that some management experts talk about generally holds true. Organizations have an echelon of top performers:

- About twenty percent of employees strongly identify with the organization, routinely give discretionary effort and are rewarded with the best bonuses, promotions and training opportunities.
- The vast majority of staff – seventy percent or so – consistently (and for the most part, efficiently) performs the requisite tasks.
- The remaining ten percent are the underperformers – employees who cause drama and seek others to blame for their unhappiness.

The idea behind building trust is to shift these numbers from 20-70-10 to something approaching 80-10-10, or even 75-25-0.

The exact number of highly engaged, moderately engaged or disengaged staff is useful as a starting point for measuring subsequent engagement numbers and because it gives leaders useful feedback on their own capabilities.

Step 2: Have "the session"

Once you have an understanding of an organization's relative engagement numbers and some of its major issues, the next step is to have a facilitated session with all employees (or a series of facilitated sessions depending on the number of employees). The facilitated session is important for a number of reasons:

- When employees have the opportunity to speak frankly about their likes and dislikes, they find it both cathartic and encouraging.
- It demonstrates leaderships' willingness to listen.
- It brings clarity to issues, usually by allowing employees to hear the rationale behind certain decisions.
- It dispels rumours, mistruths and false assumptions.
- It allows leaders to act on suggestions and gain confidence in such inclusive activities.
- It reinforces the concepts of teamwork, the organization's mission, potential opportunities and other organizational benefits (e.g., training resources).
- It reminds employees why they joined the organization in the first place.

A facilitator[106] will begin the session by establishing with participants a number of ground rules designed to focus on problem-solving rather than finger-pointing and blaming.

Participants are asked to discuss the following question:

    1. What do you like about working here?

Starting the discussions on a positive note is important; people will feel more inclined to participate and share their experiences.

    2. What needs to change to make this organization a better place to work?

This type of discussing can be quite varied, ranging from very specific suggestions to global issues. Inevitably, however, the key issues that need to be addressed will emerge. It is important to acknowledge and record each of these issues as they arise, documenting any suggestions and potential resolutions. [These will be acted on in Step 5.]

The facilitated session serves as a starting point for building organizational trust. The process actively encourages employees to contribute their thoughts and suggestions. Leaders are able to reinforce these contributions by listening actively, sharing information and providing the background and rationale for policies and decisions.

The stage is now set for an even more powerful exercise, inviting employees to help re-focus the organization.

Step 3: Establish your shared vision of excellence

ACTIVITY TIME

(1-2 hours)

RATIONALE

A shared vision of excellence (SVE) is a key first step to helping your organization define its values, prioritize resources and establish a sense of collective pride.

PROCESS

1. Using a trained facilitator, gather the organization/work unit/team into a meeting room or conference room.
2. Randomly divide the large group into discussion groups of four to five people, assigning each discussion group a flip chart or white board.
3. Have each group select its own recorder (someone to scribe the ideas) and a reporter (a person to report out to the rest of the audience).
4. Ask each discussion group to debate this question: "What is the essence of our job?"
5. Have the recorder write down the key points of the discussion on the flip chart or whiteboard.
6. At the end of the allotted time (one hour), have each discussion group develop its own shared vision of excellence (SVE). The SVE should meet the following criteria:
    - reads like a slogan and fits on a coffee cup
    - establishes priorities

- creates a sense of pride
- encourages innovation
- is consistent with organizational values, goals and missions.
7. Reconvene the entire organization/office/team and have the reporter from each group summarize their discussions and present their SVE.
8. Debate the relative merits of each proposed unifying theme (half hour).
9. Adopt one SVE for the organization (half hour). (You may have to merge two or more of the SVEs proposed by the discussion groups.)
10. Promote the SVE by incorporating it onto letterhead, e-mail tag lines, coffee cups, T-shirts, posters, etc.

OUTCOMES

Establishing a shared vision of excellence allows an organization to have a clear sense about what they do and how they do it. This knowledge gives staff more control and ownership of their work. It also enables employees to prioritize their work efficiently, manage resources more effectively and increase their level of engagement.

Why Codify Behaviour?

Other organizations attempt to influence behaviours by developing leadership competencies, codes of conduct, team charters, value statements, etc. The process of codifying acceptable employee behaviours is a valuable first step. How else can an ever-changing, diverse group of employees always know the standards for professional conduct and appropriate behaviour? How does a manager indoctrinate new hires into the corporate culture if the culture is not clearly explained, modeled and reinforced? While explaining how to behave, the development of a code of conduct (or similar document) is a futile exercise if co-workers, managers and leaders do not immediately reward appropriate behaviour – and extinguish inappropriate behaviour – consistently.

Living the Code

All successful organizations condition their employees to behave in certain ways – for example, by providing a certain level of service. For decades, IBM employees participated in public rituals celebrating corporate success, sang IBM songs and adhered to strict dress codes. The company had three core beliefs – "excellent in everything we do, superior customer service and respect for the individual" – that were reflected in the company's compensation and benefits packages, training programs and its approach to customer support.[107] Other companies use similar methods; Marriott Hotels sends new employees for "total immersion" training, track data from customer comment cards and factor it into bonuses and potential promotions. The hotel chain screens ten applicants to fill every vacancy and uses behavioural methods to reward or terminate employees. Marriott's inspectors pose as customers. If the service is good, the inspector hands the server an ID card with a $10 bill attached to it. If the service is substandard, the server receives a card that reads "Oops!" with no money attached to it. Three "Oops!" cards and the employee is let go.

A code of conduct describes the appropriate behaviours – extensive training teaches the behaviours – and bonuses, promotions, benefits and leaders reinforce them.

> **Trust Principle**
> **Successful organizations abide by a code of conduct that is created by employees, known by all and modeled by leaders.**

Step 4: Adopting a code of conduct

ACTIVITY TIME:

2-3 hours

RATIONALE

People want to contribute their talents. A staff's desire to contribute is balanced by an equally strong desire to protect oneself. If an employee experiences consistently honest and cooperative behaviours from managers and co-workers, he will reciprocate and remain highly engaged. If he perceives dishonesty, betrayal, the withholding of relevant information or other actions that limit his ability to contribute, he will become less engaged or even actively disengaged. To enable everyone to reach his or her potential, each employee must model consistency, cooperation, honesty and trustworthiness. Establishing a code of conduct reinforces key elements of trust while identifying and discouraging negative, inappropriate and counterproductive behaviours. To maximize effectiveness, the code must be visible and actively modeled by senior manages.

PROCESS

1. Using a trained facilitator, gather the entire workgroup/office/unit into a meeting room or conference room.
2. Circulate the draft code [see below].
3. Ask for everyone's input concerning the concepts, content and implications of adopting the code. Clearly communicate that everyone is expected to sign the document and adhere to its principles.
4. Agree on one code that captures the majority opinion.
5. Print and distribute the adopted code of behaviours.
6. Post the code in a prominent place; give individuals copies for their work stations and copies to new employees.

OUTCOME

A code of behaviours can be a powerful and objective way to reinforce trustworthy actions and attitudes while reducing negative, counterproductive behaviours. People will trust more quickly when such a code is continually reinforced by co-workers through bonuses and promotions and actively modeled by senior management.

Sample Code of Behaviours[cviii]

I support our shared vision of excellence, values and rules.

I will communicate with certainty.

I will speak with purpose — if it doesn't serve, I won't say it.

If I disagree or don't understand, I will ask clarifying questions.

Douglas M. Thornton

I will follow through on any commitments I make; if I can't keep a commitment, I will communicate immediately with the appropriate person and clear up any broken agreement.

I will act inclusively, sharing knowledge with co-workers, working toward solutions and being a responsible team member.

I will take personal responsibility for my actions and attitudes.

I will not engage in gossip.

Signed: _____   Date: _____

Step 5: Action!

Way back in Step 2, employees were encouraged to share their minds, thoughts and suggestions for improving the organization. Just asking is not good enough. In fact, a recent Gallup poll suggests that asking employees for feedback and then failing to act on it is demoralizing.[cix] To take the first bold step towards becoming a trust organization, it is essential to take staff suggestions, prioritize them and ask for volunteers.

Developing an Action Plan

ACTIVITY TIME:

2-3 hours

RATIONALE

Developing an action plan by involving everyone is an inclusive, positive and productive exercise that supports team building and enhances corporate communication. It capitalizes on employees' desire to contribute their skills. People are much more likely to follow through on commitments made publicly and voluntarily than when assigned tasks.

PROCESS

1. Using a trained facilitator, gather the entire work group/office/unit into a meeting room or conference room.
2. Post the suggestions from Step 2.
3. Discuss the unit's top priority tasks: "What tasks need to be done first?"
4. Ask for volunteers to perform tasks before assigning them.

5. Ask staff to form their own teams, supply due dates and suggest resources.
6. Create the action plan.

OUTCOME

A work group/office/unit gains a complete action plan that guides the key tasks for the next three to six months. Depending on the groups' wishes, a completed action plan may be circulated, posted in the conference room or even posted on an intranet site. As tasks are completed, it is important to recognize and reward contributions made by teams and individuals.

Sample Inclusive Action Plan

Task	Resource	Due Date	Completed
1) Develop a centralized calendar for the entire team.	Jeanne, Shelley, Denise	13 April 2007	✓
2) Organize, schedule and implement weekly informal staff meetings.	All	19-20 April 2007 meeting agenda action item	✓
3) Expand and modify structure of quarterly meeting to accommodate information sharing & brainstorming activities; report out action items.	Mark to develop & circulate draft agenda; Todd to record action items.	7 April 2007; 19-20 April 2007	✓
4) Develop and present draft of new employee orientation manual.	Shelley, Jeanne & Brent	Draft April; final version May 2008	
5) Mentoring proposal development	Todd	21 June 2008	

Trust...or bust?

With organizations facing unprecedented recruitment and retention challenges, private and public sector entities must explore new ways to attract and keep the best talent. An organization that models and rewards trustful behaviour at every level will be transformed into a workplace that appeals equally to employees, new staff and to customers.

By implementing the trust principles in this book, employees will become more engaged and energized. Teamwork and integrity will be valued and individuals will be encouraged to learn, apply their skills and develop their judgment. Staff will follow through on their commitments, feeling an integral part of a progressive organization with motivated people and inspiring leadership.

All of this is possible once you've built a bridge of trust.

References

Preface
[1] Diane Ford, *Trust and Knowledge Management: The Seeds of Success*, Kingston: Queen's KBE Centre for Knowledge-Based Enterprises, November 2001
[2] Organizations such as WestJet, Toyota and the Salvation Army operate on trust principles emphasizing accountability and encouraging employee initiative.
[3] Jack Welch, *Winning*, New York: HarperCollins, 2005, p.29
[4] A recent survey finding by Towers Perrin found that firms worldwide with the highest percentage of engaged employees increased operating income 19% and earnings per share 28% annually. Those firms with the lowest employee engagement scores showed year-to-year *declines* in operating income of 33% and in earnings per share 11%. (Source: National Post, 24 October 2007, p. WK5)

Chapter 1-- The Trust Principles
[5] provided these behaviours are reinforced and periodically rewarded
[6] In their ground-breaking book *Funky Business: Talent Makes Capital Dance,* Swedish economists Kjell Nordstrom and Jonas Ridderstrale argue convincingly that talent, imagination and innovation are the critical determinants of commercial success.
[7] Jack Welsh, *Winning*, p.15.
[8] "Saving the Business Without Losing the Company", Harvard Business Review, January 2002, p. 42
[9] Louis V. Gerstner, *Who Says Elephants Can't Dance?*, New York: HarperBusiness 2002, p. 236
[10] The Ontario Ministry of Education has a code of conduct, as do lobbyists involved with the Government of Canada. Corporate examples are shown at www.ibe.org.uk/examples.html.
[11] Gerald H. Seijts, Cases in Organizational Behaviour, quoted from
http://books.google.com/books?id=P85wUZKfKVAC&pg=P

A60&lpg=PA60&dq=westjet+management+team+cleaning+planes&source=web&ots=M4JM_dYi1x&sig=7M9kjWabroPmRq3Q4-znhv9jG1w#PPA1,M1

[12] Robert A. Watson and Ben Brown, *Leadership Secrets of the Salvation Army* (New York: Crown Business, 2001), p.106

[13] Participant's comments, 26 September 2006, Building Trust for Managers© Workshop, Toronto ON

[14] Pierre Berton, "The secrets of the Vimy success," Globe and Mail, 4 April 2007

[15] www.civilization.ca/cwm/vimy/index_e.html

[16] http://www.brainyquote.com/quotes/authors/a/albert_einstein.htm

Chapter 2-- Changing Organizational Culture

[17] Welch, *Winning*, pp. 31-32

Chapter 3-- Problems in the Workplace

[18] The survey defines employee engagement as "the measure of people's willingness and ability to give discretionary effort at work."

[19] Paul Luke, CanWest News Service, "Burned-out boomers retiring while on the job" www.canada.com/components

[20] "New research shows workforce productivity gains exaggerated" www.convergys.com/news_release.php?y=2004&q=3&newsid=2050

[21] www.insurance-canada.ca/market/canada/Ipsos-Health-Productivity-507.php

[22] The Exxon Valdez oil spill acted as a catalyst for greater environmental protection initiatives. www.epa.gov/oilspill/exxon.htm

[23] David Allen, *Getting Things Done,* New York: Penguin Group, 2002.

[24] In smaller organizations, some of these functions are outsourced.

Chapter 4-- The Trust Organization

[25] "The modern multinational corporation was invented in 1859." "Peter Drucker on Leadership" www.forbes.com, 19 November 2004

[26] There are some exceptions to this in the last decade or so, e.g. attitudinal-based hiring and behavioural based interviewing.

[27] Y. Malhotra, "Business Process Re-design: An Overview," IEEE Engineering Magazine, vol. 26, no. 3., Fall 1998

[28] J. Richard Hackman, *Leading Teams: Setting the Stage of Great Performances* (Boston: Harvard School Business Press), p. 38

[29] Student scores in North America show a steady decline in linguistic abilities and other basic literacy and communications skills.

[30] Conference Board of Canada's ninth biennial survey of Canadian organizations

[31] "Violence at Work in North America," North American Commission for Labor Cooperation, published by the Secretariat of the Commission for Labor Cooperation, 2006

[32] Linda Duxbury and Chris Higgins, "Work/Life Balance in the New Millennium: Where are we? Where do we need to go?", CPRN Discussion Paper #12, October 2001

[33] Peter F. Drucker, *The Essential Drucker* (New York: HarperCollins, 2001), p.16

[34] Welch, *Winning*, p.113

[35] Mike Johnson and Ryan Walter, *Simply the Best: Insights and Strategies from Great Hockey Coaches*, (Surrey: Heritage House Publishing, 2004), p. 162

[36] For example, *The Speed of Trust* by Stephen Covey, *Organizational Trust: A Reader* (Oxford Management Readers) and Robert M. Galford's *The Trusted Leader* to name a few.

[37] www.cambridgetourism.com/sub/Toyota/default.asp

[38] www.clickz.com/showPage.html?page=3367181

Chapter 5-- Trust Organization vs. the Average Organization

[39] All of the examples for the "average organization" are taken from organizations of 5,000+ employees and are based on interviews, questionnaires and survey results.

[40] www.iveybusinessjournal.com/view_article.asp?intArticle_ID=616

[41] www.iveybusinessjournal.com/view_article.asp?intArticle_ID=616

[42] This is not just rhetoric – 87% of employees spend an average of 13% of their salaries purchasing WestJet stock.

[43] www.albertapork.com/producers/whjournal/WHJ-2004-03(Banff)/Staying%20Competitive

[44] www.cbc.ca/money/story/2004/08/03/westJet_040803.html

[45] Ipsos Reid Surveys of BC and Ontario civil services, 2006

[46] www.management-issues.com/2006/8/24/research/senior-executives-lack-communications-skills.asp

[47] "Only 6% feel valued by the boss," National Post, 24 October 2007, p. WK5

[48] The value of the Dow Jones Industrial Average has increased from approximately 750 to 11,000 from 1980-2007. www.margin-call.net/wykresyhistoryczne/djia1.html

[49] Joe Nocera, "Rolling in it," National Post, 24 October 2007, p. WK6

[50] www.discoverysurveys.com/articles/itw-026.html

[51] Tom Peters, *Thriving on Chaos: Handbook for a Management Revolution*, see http://itre.cis.upenn.edu/~myl/languagelog/archives/002964.html

[52] Seymour M. Hersh, "The Stovepipe," New Yorker, October 27, 2003

[53] http://science.ksc.nasa.gov/shuttle/missions/51-l/docs/rogers-commission/Chapter-6.txt

[54] http://globeandmail.com, "Trust is improving in workplaces, survey finds", 26 September 2006.

Chapter 6-- The "Feel" of Trust

[55] The cost to replace Brenda is estimated to be between 100 and 150% of her annual salary.
[56] Teresa Amabile and Steven Kramer, "Inner Work Life" Harvard Business Review, May 2007, pp. 72-83.
[57] Arky Ciancutti and Thomas Steding, "Trust Fund", Business 2.0, 13 June 2000.
[58] Of 5,000 working Canadians surveyed in 2007, only 6% felt valued by their managers and only 23% felt engaged in their work. National Post, 24 October 2007

Chapter 7—The Good News: Workplace Trust Already Exists

[59] "Code of Values and Behaviours for Leaders," Ministry of Finance, Province of Ontario, 2006
[60] J. Richard Hackman, *Leading Teams* (Boston: Harvard Business School Press, 2002)
[61] "Birds of a Feather Flock Together...at Work: New Survey Points to Productivity Gains When Friends Work Together," www.accountemps.com/portal/site/at-us/template, 14 June 2007
[62] *Simply the Best*, p.58.
[63] *Simply the Best*, p. 165
[64] "Up Front: Executive Interview with Sean Durfy," Canadian Business Magazine, 23 April 2007, p.14

Chapter 8-- The Bad News: Barriers to Trust Exist

[65] *Built to Last*, p. 3
[66] *Built to Last*, pp. 128-9
[67] Built to *Last*, pp. 135-7
[68] "BC Stats", 2006 Work Environment Survey results
[69] http://dsp-psd.pwgsc.gc.ca/Collection/GomeryII/RestoringAccountability-Recommendations/CISPAA_Report_Chapter5.pdf
According to a Report on the Responsibilities and Accountabilities of Deputy Ministers, deputies serve lass than 3.5 years' tenure, "...too short a time for a deputy minister to fully understand the programs, policies and administration of a department; to take effective control of its management; ...to live with the consequences of his or her decisions. This same problem of too-brief tenure in

office exists at the level of assistant deputy minister. " p. 109

[70] Gomery Commission, pp.105-06

[71] Ibid. p. 107. While this report deals with federal civil servants, the same criticisms apply to most of their provincial government counterparts.

[72] Chris Thatcher and Paul Crookall, "Answering the Call: Who Will Fill the Management Void?" 13 December 2007, Canadian Government Executive Magazine

[73] defined as having fewer than 50 employees or operated by a self-employed person with no paid help. http://www.bcstats.gov.bc.ca/data/bus_stat/busind/sm_bus/SBP2007.pdfBC Stats, "Small Business Profile 2007"

[74] "Canadian Business Goes Global for Growth?" TD Bank Financial Group, June 2004, p. 7 http://www.tdcanadatrust.com/smallbusiness/pdf/economics_june04.pdf

[75] Infoline, BC Stats, Issue 07-47, 23 November 2007, p. 1

[76] An employee's perception of a workplace event dictates levels of engagement and motivation. While an employee's perception of an event is subjective and may appear skewed to you or me, the fact remains that it can become an insurmountable obstacle negatively affecting morale and productivity.

Chapter 9-- Overcoming Communication Barriers

[77] http://c3dsp.westjet.com/guest/about/ownersCampaignTemplate.jsp

[78] Walkerton, Ontario, a small agricultural town of about 5,000, suffered a terrible tragedy in 2000 when seven people died, dozens were hospitalized and hundreds suffered from a deadly outbreak of E. coli contamination in the town's water supply. The episode was caused by the negligence of the town's environmental health inspector, who failed to test the town's water supply properly. In economic terms, the loss was estimated at $160 M. http://canadaonline.about.com/gi/dynamic/offsite.htm?site=http://www.cbc.ca/news/background/walkerton/

[79] For a comprehensive discussion on the concept and benefits of using 10% closure, see Ciancutti, Arky and Steding Thomas, *Built on Trust : Gaining Competitive*

Advantage in Any Organization (Chicago: Contemporary Books, 2001).
[80] "Saving the Business without Losing the Company", Harvard Business Review, January 2002, p. 42.

Chapter 10-- Managing People
[81] "No.1 Reason People Quit Their Jobs" http://webcenters.netscape.compuserve.com/whatsnew/package.jsp?name=fte/quitjobs/quitjobs&floc=wn-dx
[82] "Can Employees Be Friends With the Boss?" http://gmj.gallup.com/content/23893/Can-Employees-Be-Friends-With-the-Boss.aspx
[83] Collins, James and Porras, Jerry, *Built to Last: Successful Habits of Visionary Companies* (New York: HarperCollins Publishing), pp. 1-11.
[84] There is no shortage of examples of unsuccessful leaders or for the myriad of reasons why they failed. See Andrew Roberts' *Hitler and Churchill: Secrets of Leadership* (London: Phoenix Books, 2004) for an interesting look at personality and leadership.
[85] http://www.scu.edu/ethics/dialogue/candc/cases/worldcom.html
[86] http://goliath.ecnext.com/coms2/gi_0199-194362/Behind-closed-doors-at-WorldCom.html
[87] http://www.cbc.ca/news/background/worldcom/
[88] "Former WorldCom Auditor Describes Whistle-blowing," http://www.webcpa.com/article.cfm?articleid=25779
[89] For a recent look at owner/manager dynamics, see http://www.grantthornton.ca/surveys/Owner-Manager-Digest.pdf
[90] Clive Beddoes' successor at WestJet is Sean Durfy. Durfy is credited with establishing the "owner's care" campaign currently defining the organization's culture.
[91] Management guru Peter Drucker estimated that between 3 and 5% of all businesses are "well managed." http://findarticles.com/p/articles/mi_m4153/is_n4_v55/ai_21119266
[92] "Is Your Boss a Psychopath?" http://www.fastcompany.com/magazine/96/open_boss.html

[93] Steven B. Sample, *The Contrarian's Guide to Leadership*, San Francisco: Jossey-Bass, 2002 , p. 190
[94] BC Stats, "Work Environment Survey 2006," p. 5

Chapter 11—Barriers to Trust: Lack of Personal Accountability

[95] Although the policy was largely supported by war-weary populations mired in economic depression, naïveté concerning Nazi Germany's expansionist aspirations ultimately prevented Britain and France from taking decisive steps to rearm, preventing Germany from rearming and forcing Hitler to fight before he achieved his near military superiority.
[96] Welch, *Winning*, p. 63
[97] Gerstner, *Who Says Elephants Can't Dance?*, pp. 208-9
[98] "Peter Drucker on Making Decisions," http://hbswk.hbs.edu/archive/4208.html
[99] Duxbury cites familiar examples of governments and the RCMP in "Win Hearts of Mounties to Revive Force, Expert Says," http://www.dose.ca/news/story.html?id=b3b50735-a893-4ade-b789-c686c62530af

[100] "Air Canada emerges from bankruptcy protection", http://www.cbc.ca/money/story/2004/09/30/aircan_09 3004.html
[101] "The Survey Says Air Canada has a Severe Morale Problem", http://www.ccnmattews.com/news, 8 November 2006.
[102] "Academic survey of Air Canada Pilots finds Morale Extremely Low", http://flyertalk.com/forum/archive/index.php/t-721560.html
[103] "Medicine: The Unhappy Profession?", http://www.cmaj.ca/cgi/content/full/168/6/751
[104] "Study: We All Tell Lies Over the Phone", http://abcnews.go.com/Technology/story?id=99576

Chapter 12

[105] An excellent investment with an estimated ROI of 9:1, see http://www.bcpublicservice.ca/learning/pdf/Corporate%20Learning%20Strategy.pdf

[106] In a recent study conducted by the Harvard Graduate School of Education, groups using a trained facilitator produced 600% more ideas than those without one.

[107] Gerstner, *Who Says Elephants Can't Dance?*, pp. 184-5

[cviii] Adapted from Jack Canfield, The Success Principles: How to Get from Where You Are to Where You Want to Be (New York, HarperCollins, 2005), p. 363

[cix] "You've Gotten Employee Feedback, Now What?" Gallup Management Journal, 11 May 2006.

ISBN 1425168193